how to narrow your focus
and grow your small business
with social media

niche, please!

skyler irvine

LIONCREST
PUBLISHING

NICHE, PLEASE!

How to Narrow Your Focus and Grow Your
Small Business with Social Media

ISBN   978-1-5445-2174-9 *Hardcover*
      978-1-5445-2173-2 *Paperback*
      978-1-5445-2172-5 *Ebook*

To my wife Lizy, who is proof that it's up to us to make the life we want. And to my kids, who inspire me to be more curious about all aspects of life, especially outside of the office.

Contents

Part I

Get Ready to Niche

CHAPTER 1

Do Less, Achieve More

There's a lot of noise out there: Facebook, Twitter, Instagram, Snapchat, LinkedIn, TikTok, Tumblr, Pinterest.

I could go on, but then I'd just be adding to the noise.

If you're a current small-business owner, or you're considering taking a first dive into entrepreneurship, you know there's some sort of magic with social media. Supposedly, everything you need to start or expand your business is just on the other side of some app. But there's so much to worry about. *Should I blog, or should I start a podcast? Should I use Instagram, Facebook, or LinkedIn? And what's up with how these "algorithms" work?* All this noise can make a new, or even seasoned, entrepreneur feel as if they're starting from zero—as if they could never possibly learn enough about social media to effectively use it to grow the reach of their business.

But I have a secret for you, and if you hear nothing else, hear this:

You're already 80 to 90 percent there.

Your new (or current) business isn't on stage zero; it's closer to stage eight or nine. Your fresh ideas, your creativity, your connections, your skills, your services, your products, your relationships, your insider's knowledge, all combine to create something that no person, no business, no expert marketer anywhere in the world can ever offer:

You.

You are the secret weapon that literally no competitor can ever replicate. In business, something that no one else has is called a monopoly. I call it a superpower.

This book isn't going to change everything about you. Instead, it will hopefully be the guide you need to super-charge your already present skills. You're finally going to discover the tools—and the confidence—to share your unique business with the world in a way that's unstoppable.

Sound too good to be true?

It's not.

I help small-business owners and new entrepreneurs narrow their focus and grow their reach. And when both of those happen, the owner watches as their business grows, and they discover exciting new opportunities they may never have imagined. Importantly, I help people take what they're already good at—their current businesses and their creative ideas for new businesses—and then I show them how social media can supercharge those ventures. Often, after I help a client start their first social media campaign, they say, "Wow. *That's* what I was so afraid of?!"

That's how you'll feel by the end of this book.

I started writing this book in 2019, while enjoying a flourishing marketplace with low unemployment. A few months later, everything changed with the COVID-19 global pandemic. Besides the health impact, the economy was devastated. Skilled workers were laid off. Hardworking, educated singles lost their jobs. Moms and dads were out of work. People everywhere with amazing ideas and incredible skills were suddenly left unemployed.

I knew then—and still know, now—that people only lost their jobs, not their superpowers. And I don't believe in throwing away superpowers. As scary as a pandemic, a recession, or unemployment can be, these scenarios also create opportunity and motivation. Often, scary times are exactly what we need to push us into our long-held dreams. Here's what I want for those who find themselves unemployed or simply unfulfilled:

I want Mom to take her real estate skills online.

I want Dad to use his teaching certificate on the web.

I want someone to stop listening to podcasts and finally start their own.

I want everyone with a fresh business idea to have the courage to take on the giants within their industry.

I know these are all possible, because a few years before all this, I was in a similar scenario. I had skills, but I needed to sprinkle some magic in with those skills.

After graduating college in 2007, I had just enough time to look for, find, and get fired from my first job, just before the 2008 financial crisis. So, I started looking at the real estate market, and I came up with a plan to buy foreclosed homes at auction, hold them until the market corrected, and resell them. Luckily, the market corrected in less time than I had even imagined, and I started seeing profits from purchasing foreclosed homes almost immediately. But after I had bought and resold over sixty homes, the prices at auction suddenly doubled. Apparently, a multi-billion-dollar private equity firm liked my strategy, so they moved into my area and copied my model on a larger scale. My margins were gone, along with my business model.

I may have been out of a job, essentially unemployed, but I still had unique skills and expertise (just like you do).

I decided to pivot my real estate company; instead of buying foreclosed homes and reselling them, I would help others buy homes. *But how do I get the word out about my new real estate company?* I thought.

That's when I discovered the power of social media, which became the magic ingredient that supercharged my real estate skills.

SOCIAL MEDIA = SKILLS SUPERCHARGED

In 2011, no real estate agent thought Facebook was anything more than a fun way to keep up with distant relatives and high school sweethearts. But it was perfect for me and my new real estate business. It allowed me to use all the things I was best at, without becoming someone I wasn't. It allowed me to post personal content about myself, my interests, and my hobbies, and when applicable, I posted real estate content. This one social media tool put all my other skills and experiences into hyperdrive and transformed my real estate business. While I was spending all my marketing budget ($0) and all my marketing focus on one place (the right social media platform), my real estate competitors spread their efforts like crazy across every marketing effort—bus benches, grocery carts, printed mailers, billboards, TV ads, and a haphazard collection of social media platforms they barely understood. Meanwhile, I invested my time and effort into the niche place that fit with me, my business, and my customers: Facebook. I didn't need to go viral and reach every person—I just needed to reach the right clients.

Notice I learned one social medium, not 200. Also, I didn't become a videography expert, a photography expert, or even an expert at all other forms of social media.

And that's a lesson that every new entrepreneur or current business owner will be happy to hear:

To supercharge your business with social media, you don't need to do more.

You actually need to do *less*.

Instead of going wider, you need to go deeper. You don't need to reach *more* people—you need to reach more of the *right* people. You don't need to sell a larger variety of services or products. You need to sell more of your best-selling services or products. If you're a new entrepreneur, you just need to sell plenty of that one great idea you've been sitting on. You don't need to learn more about dozens of social media marketing platforms. You just need to learn about one platform that's right for you, your business, your skills, and your customer.

> To supercharge your business with social media, you don't need to do more.
>
> You actually need to do *less*.

To put it simply, you need to narrow your focus to grow your reach.

At my new real estate business, once I narrowed my focus onto skills I already had and the work I truly enjoyed (connecting with customers), I began to ask myself, *Could I help others do the same: narrow their business focus and grow their reach using social media?*

It turns out, the answer is yes.

In 2015 I pivoted again. I left the real estate business and founded RenzlerMedia to help other small businesses do what I had done for myself in real estate—find big opportunities in small niches and capitalize on changing trends.

Today, in 2021, I've helped dozens of entrepreneurs and

businesses find success using a variety of social media and digital content.

Social media, and all of digital marketing, have evolved rapidly and often since I started selling real estate. Instagram has taken the visual world by storm, podcasting has emerged as a global phenomenon, and TikTok has entered the national spotlight. There will be more changes tomorrow. But I've used all these trends and more to help entrepreneurs and businesses supercharge their skills, narrow their focus, and grow their reach.

It's time for you to do the same.

By holding this book, you're holding the key to conquering your fear of social media, utilizing the skills you already have, and putting them to use in an online era. Whether you're a dancer, a B2B business, a CPA, a boutique apparel brand, a teacher, a creator, or an artist, this book will show you how to monetize your skillset and capitalize on the digital world so you can supercharge your talents. And there's no need to worry about not being able to handle social media. I know you can do it, because you've already learned one big lesson:

To supercharge your business with social media, you don't need to do more. You actually need to do less.

Now, get ready to niche—please.

SUMMARY

You don't need to do more. You actually need to do less as an entrepreneur. Often, social media intimidates entrepreneurs. But that's only because they don't have a guidebook. Now, you're holding one. And the best news is, I'm here to tell you that social media marketing isn't going to make your life any harder. I'm here to help you do less and achieve more.

Key takeaways:

- Social media supercharges your skills. Using social media marketing doesn't mean you should change yourself. In fact, when used correctly, social media marketing simply helps take your natural talents and supercharge them.
- You just completed an entire chapter about social media. See how hard that *wasn't*? That's exactly the level of difficulty you can expect in the rest of this book. You got this.

CHAPTER 2

"Everything's Changed!"

I know what you're thinking, and it's probably what you would be saying to me right now if we were having this discussion live:

"Skyler, social media has changed everything about running a business today. We've never seen anything like this before."

But we have seen changes like social media before. And smart businesses and entrepreneurs not only survived, but they also took advantage of that change, and you can too.

Let's journey back to a time where smartphones, internet, and television were all absent, but gender stereotypes were prevalent.

Let's go back to the 1930s.

Middle-class men across America worked while house-wives stayed home, cleaning, cooking, and raising children. Women made decisions on household goods, which meant that household brands wanted their attention.

In the previous decade—the 1920s—Procter & Gamble, Colgate, and other household brands gained attention by advertising in various newspapers. That's how marketing had been done for decades: if you wanted to gain some-one's attention, you did it with a print ad in a newspaper.

But then radio happened.

Alone on the weekdays, women started tuning in to hear their favorite daytime radio shows. *Bachelor's Children, Backstage Wife, Betty and Bob, Ma Perkins,* and on and on. Each of these shows was packed, episode by episode, with family and women's issues, and of course there was lots of drama. Each episode ended on a cliffhanger, prompting excited listeners to tune into the next one. These shows held women's attention—the same attention household brands wanted. So, what did household brands do? The smart brands, instead of fighting the change, joined the new media by sponsoring and producing the shows, plastering their brand name across the new and dramatic storytelling medium. Oxydol, Super Suds, Double Danderine, Bab-O,

Easy-Off, and dozens of other soaps and cleaning products became synonymous with these radio shows. Few realized it then, but when brands started sponsoring these daytime radio shows they were ushering in a new type of content. Today, we refer to these dramatic shows, originally funded and sponsored mostly by branded soaps, as soap operas.

In one sense, the radio offered a new type of media that appeared to differ greatly from the old way of marketing in newspapers. You can imagine the mad men of the day discussing it:

"How will we ever learn to market on the *radio*?"

"Radio is too new, too complicated."

"We'll never understand how to advertise with *sound*."

On one hand, the mad men were right. Radio changed how consumers were spending their attention. The home radio meant brands had to reconsider marketing tactics. They had to leap off the printed newspaper page. They had to learn about audio and sound recordings. They had to incorporate the stars of the soap operas directly into their brand messaging.

But that was just one side of the coin, and it's usually the only side people focus on.

The other truth is this: radio marketing didn't change "everything." Brands still retained their skills and, in general, continued to produce and sell their same products. They still retained everything they had learned about their customers from their previous years of running their businesses. They still had creative, fresh ideas about what to offer.

Plus, their products didn't change. They still sold soaps. Radio barely affected that.

Lastly, the rule of marketing never changed. Marketing still boiled down to one thing—attention—and advertising on radio via soap operas was simply a different way to gain the same attention.

When you look at the scenario with all that in mind, radio didn't change *everything*.

Yes, some companies were left in the dust, because they focused on the difficulty, rather than the opportunity, of radio. They saw radio as a major overhaul, an obstacle, something to fear. But one company in particular went all-in on this new media platform and eventually dominated the soap opera genre, sponsoring shows all the way into the 2010s. That company is Procter & Gamble, which today is pulling in about $70 billion a year, and worth almost $300 billion. Procter & Gamble still sells household brands, many of which are marketed to women. They remained true to themselves when radio happened; they just flexed their marketing plan to respond to changing attention.

So, yes, radio forever changed the game of marketing.

But then TV did it again in the 1950s.

In the 1990s, the internet took over.

In the 2000s, YouTube video took over.

In the 2010s, Instagram became the marketing king.

In the 2020s, TikTok started spreading from device to device at an unprecedented pace.

Oh, and by 2030, the hottest platform will be...

I don't know yet, but I do know this:

We've been here before, and each new medium is simply a different way to gain the same attention.

THE THREE NICHES YOU NEED

Procter & Gamble recognized that radio changed how women spent their attention, but it didn't change their business model. They just considered their own offerings in light of the market opportunity of the home radio. The result was that they helped develop a new kind of storytelling, called soap operas, which they added to their existing skills of selling soaps and other household goods. They deployed this new type of storytelling on radio channels.

And we can all copy Procter & Gamble's process. When you break it down, Procter & Gamble followed a three-niche approach:

1. Business Niche: they narrowly focused on selling soaps to women.
2. Content Niche: they developed a specific type of audio content called soap operas for a specific group of people.
3. Media Niche: they deployed their new soap operas through the most obvious method—radio channels.

Every business, every current and new entrepreneur, can use this same three-niche approach to maximize their business and marketing opportunities.

BIZ-NICHE

Business is selling. So, a business *niche* is simply selling, but selling specifically. Saying "I sell everything to everyone!" sounds nice. Yes: perhaps later you can focus on selling everything to everyone, but that is not a good place to start.

Lasers work on this basic premise: a conglomeration of otherwise low-power light waves coming together at one point to create enhanced, robust ability. That's exactly what finding a business niche—or a Biz-Niche, as I like to call it—can do for you. A Biz-Niche allows you to pull all your business energy into one point to target your future customers. Essentially, the more you narrow your business focus, the more power you have. This type of narrowing helps increase your power and your profit margins, find your customers, and reduce competition. It explains why Walmart sells $200 bicycles to everyone and REI sells $5,000 mountain bikes specifically to competitive mountain bikers. A Biz-Niche can also take a general dance teacher to a ballet teacher who sells premium lessons to advanced fourteen- to sixteen-year-old dancers who hope to turn pro. A Biz-Niche could also be geography-specific. For instance, a high-end real estate company in Manhattan would be using geography as part of their Biz-Niche.

You can put all these elements together to help you find *your* Biz-Niche: the narrow focus of selling your product or service to a subcategory of people with low competition.

> Your Biz-Niche: the narrow focus of selling your product or service to a subcategory of people with low competition.

CONTENT NICHE

A Content Niche is simply the specific type of content you produce directed at your customer. Many small-business owners and entrepreneurs get overwhelmed by all the available types of social media and digital marketing. They see blogs, vlogs, video, and other content types, and it's just too much, and they don't have time for all of it. So, they put someone else in charge of their marketing (for some reason, it's always their favorite niece). While the favorite niece may understand aspects of social media, the business owner rarely gets involved enough to explain the business to her. So, she does her best, but with little direction, she spreads her efforts thin. The results are lackluster.

I knew social media marketing was a waste, thinks the owner.

But the problem isn't social media, and it definitely isn't the niece. The problem is lack of strategy.

That's why you need your own Content Niche: the specific type of content you create, based on you, your business, your customer, minus the competition.

Instead of overwhelming an entrepreneur with the prospect of making a hundred different types of content, a Content Niche focuses on one content. It pushes you to start by focusing on only one type of content, like a video series or microblogging directed at your customer.

> Your Content Niche: the specific type of content you create, based on you, your business, your customer, minus the competition.

Here's the best part: you get to be you. To find the right Content Niche, you get to dive into what you like most about your company and your customers.

In this book, we'll look at any special skills you or your business has. Then, we'll look at your current or future customer and where they spend their attention. Finally, we'll consider the available market opportunities. When you put all of that into the mix, you can then concentrate on one Content Niche. You'll know what type of content you (and/or your company) should create, and you'll know what to post, because it will all track to a strategy.

That's why the soap operas were such a hit, and why Procter & Gamble won: they didn't have to keep recreating the wheel. Once they focused their efforts on the perfect type of content for them and their customer, they kept producing what they knew their customer would love. You probably don't need to invent a totally new type of content like soap operas, although you could if you wanted. Your Content Niche could be as simple as a blog or posting pictures online, as long as they're directed at the right group of people. And the right Content Niche isn't necessarily the one that's the shiniest. The right choice is the one that's easy and fun for you and your company to consistently produce and that enables you to gain the attention of your customer.

MEDIA NICHE

A Media Niche is simply *where* you post your content. For Procter & Gamble, it was pretty obvious that their soap operas would be "posted" on radio channels, at least at first. (Later, Procter & Gamble pivoted, and actually changed both their Content and Media Niches to create *visual* soap operas, which they put on television.)

While not every company needs to use social media to post their content and gain the attention of their customers, this book is geared toward the small-business owner and entrepreneur for whom social media is a gold mine. So, for our purposes in this book, this is how we will define *your* Media Niche: the specific social media platform where you post your content. (Although, technically, in a broader sense, a Media Niche could include traditional media, such as billboards, radio, and television.)

> Your Media Niche: the specific social media platform where you post your content.

THE THREE NICHES OF DOLLAR SHAVE CLUB

You can find this three-niche approach popping up in most successful businesses. The Dollar Shave Club (DSC) is an excellent modern-day example of how the three niches operate, and how social media helps the little guy. In 2012, Gillette was the Goliath in the men's razor blade category, owning the lion's share of the razor blade maker in the United States.

But then DSC happened.

While Gillette was pouring millions into its ongoing television advertising, such as over-produced Super Bowl commercials, DSC had a different plan. They narrowed their focus onto selling inexpensive razors to men between sixteen and twenty-four years of age. DSC knew that men rarely change brands, so if they captured men early, DSC would become part of their buying habits as men aged.

A NOTE ON SELLING CONTENT

If you're a content creator who sells the content itself, not just uses it for marketing purposes, then your niches may overlap so much that they are nearly the same thing. For instance, if you sell e-books, then your Biz-Niche and Content Niche may look pretty similar. Even in that case, this book could revolutionize the way you spend your time and energy by focusing your efforts on what's most effective. Keep reading.

As far as content goes, DSC looked into their toolbox. One, they weren't fancy, so they didn't try to be fancy. Two, the founder is a bit sarcastic, so they used sarcasm. Three, they didn't have a huge budget to compete with Gillette on television, so they needed something cheap.

So DSC doubled down on their superpowers and created un-fancy, sarcastic, low-budget video content. And where do you post that kind of content? YouTube.

One of their videos—titled *Our Blades Are F***ing Great*—cost just $4,500 and took a single day to shoot, and went viral on YouTube in 2012. When it did, DSC exploded. Soon, they were doing hundreds of millions in revenue, and handily stealing market share from Gillette.

Did you catch DSC's three niches?

Biz-Niche: selling inexpensive razors to men between sixteen and twenty-four years old.

Content Niche: underproduced, sarcastic, low-budget videos, directed at men who buy razors.

Media Niche: YouTube.

This three-niche approach worked for DSC, which ended up selling to Unilever in 2016 for $1 billion.

That's the power of the three niches coming together on social media. They give the Davids of the world a chance to get in the game and fight the Goliath businesses who stand in their way.

Be like DSC.

NARROW FOCUS ≠ BEING STUCK

Maybe you're thinking, *If I niche down, I'll be stuck.*

Let's tackle that misconception.

Creative people, like entrepreneurs, often believe that if they niche down, they're thinking too small. But that's an unrealistic scarcity mindset instead of the abundance mindset that the marketplace truly offers. In particular, narrowing the focus of your Biz-Niche is, perhaps ironically, the first step to growing your reach.

Consider Under Armour. They didn't start out as a general clothing company. They started out selling one sports apparel product—compression shirts for underneath football pads. Talk about niche. That narrow focus enabled Under Armour to create and dominate one product. From there, they eventually expanded and became a primary challenger to Nike's long-standing hold in the sports apparel world in almost every genre, from golf, to football, to basketball, to baseball and beyond.

Lululemon has a similar story—their Biz-Niche was selling high-end workout leggings to women. Lululemon's dominance, energy, and focus created such an effect that their main product spilled out into pop culture. Today, you can go almost anywhere in public life and find their brand's effect, as women, and a growing number of men, go about their daily lives in a new type of clothing called "athleisure." And Lululemon hasn't stopped. Having dominated and expanded their original category, the company has moved into handbags, belts, yoga mats, men's clothing, dress shirts, and water bottles. They even purchased Mirror, an innovative in-home workout training program.

Even DSC has expanded from their original niche. They now offer everything from razors to toothpaste to hair products.

So don't let the "I'll be stuck if I niche" thought stick in your head. It's completely false.

~~~~~

Okay, so it's time to find your three niches: your Biz-Niche, Content Niche, and Media Niche. By the end of this book, you'll have all three, and you'll have conquered the fear of social media. Go find that first niche, please!

SUMMARY

We've been here before. While it may feel like social media is new, it's simply the next step in the evolution of marketing. Marketing has relentlessly changed throughout human history, from print ads, to radio, to television, to social media. It will certainly change again. When marketing changes, your core business products and services can largely remain the same, as long as you maintain your customer's attention as necessary.

Key takeaways:

- Successful companies focus on three niches. You should, too!
- Your Biz-Niche: the narrow focus of selling your product or service to a subcategory of people with low competition.

- Your Content Niche: the specific type of content you create, based on you, your business, your customer, minus the competition.
- Your Media Niche: the specific social media platform where you post your content.
- Narrow focus does not equate to being stuck. Perhaps counterintuitively, narrowing your focus is the first step to expansion. Remember Under Armour, Lululemon, and DSC; all three of these businesses niched down at first, then later exploded.

Part II

Your Biz-Niche

CHAPTER 3

The Biz-Niche Formula

Owning a business is hard.

Increased competition, market saturation, and lots of noise can make running a business very difficult. Starting, expanding, and simply surviving require tenacity, as businesses must push through a crowded marketplace of similar offerings in money-tight arenas.

That's exactly where Lizy found herself in the mid-2000s, when she became a licensed loan officer.

While most people are familiar with how real estate agents get paid, few understand the complexities of the mortgage process, so here's a quick summary:

Whenever customer Jane is ready to purchase a home, she'll need a loan officer to help her apply for and get the home-loan money from a lender, like Bank of America (unless she's paying cash). Jane probably handpicks her real estate agent, but likely, she doesn't know any loan officers. Instead, Jane will just ask her real estate agent: "Hey, I need a loan officer to help me get approved for a home loan. Who should I use?" Jane's real estate agent will then refer their favorite loan officer, because no house gets sold, and no one gets paid, if Jane doesn't get the cash she needs to purchase the home. That's why real estate agents often keep recommending their clients (like Jane) to the same, trusted loan officers, over and over again. The real estate agent wants to make sure the loan gets approved so they get their commission. This embedded referral process can make it difficult for new loan officers to gain any traction.

Lizy had just finished her loan officer licensing, and unlike most of her established competitors, she didn't have a decade of working relationships with real estate agents. She found herself swimming in a sea of experienced loan officer sharks. Real estate agents weren't interested in using a new loan officer. So, Lizy found her own Biz-Niche. Or, actually, her Biz-Niche found her.

At the time, because of the boom in real estate, most loan officers had *their* pick of which homebuyers to work with. It was simple supply and demand: there were so many easy applications that most loan officers wanted nothing to do with harder loan applications that required more time.

And what did young and broke Lizy have plenty of in 2005?

Time.

Lizy found a Biz-Niche by working exclusively with qualified buyers whose loans required extra time and more work.

For the next three years, she grinded it out with harder-than-average applications. Eventually, she developed a reputation among real estate agents as the go-to loan officer for well-qualified but atypical homebuyers. Even other loan officers started sending difficult applicants directly to Lizy. In this way she found a Biz-Niche, and therefore, business success.

Then in 2008, everything changed.

The housing bubble popped, and demand diminished. Home prices fell, banking regulations stiffened, and there was no such thing as an "easy" loan application anymore. Most experienced loan officers felt completely lost with a rapidly changing market and new regulations.

But Lizy was right at home. She quickly became the go-to person for any loan application, because, when the rules tightened, every application required extra steps. Everyone wanted, and needed, her expertise. She began taking on more and more clients over the next few years, while other loan officers lost theirs or chose to abandon the industry altogether.

Her business accelerated, built upon years of niching down on one area, until, in 2018, Lizy was ranked as the number-one female loan officer in the country by the Scotsman Guide (a popular publication in the mortgage industry).

She entered a very crowded marketplace, established her Biz-Niche, and doubled down. Her niche expertise outgrew itself, and Lizy became a powerhouse for her entire industry. She would have succeeded in any market because she is an excellent loan officer, but by narrowing her focus, she maximized her efforts. When you do that, you win, period. Also, if the marketplace happens to tilt in your favor, as it did with Lizy, you might win really big, putting your already-successful Biz-Niche into hyperdrive.

And that's the power of finding a Biz-Niche.

Be like Lizy.

~~~~~

Entrepreneurs can find useful takeaways from Lizy's experience, if they lean in and pay attention. That's particularly easy for me to do, because Lizy Hoeffer Irvine is my wife.

THE BIZ-NICHE FORMULA

Whether it was intentional or not, Lizy used a formula to find her Biz-Niche. Every business can utilize this concept, regardless of size or industry.

It's a simple formula:

WHO	Who do you want to reach with your product or service?
WHAT	What action(s) do you want them to take?
WHY	Why would they choose you over the competition?
YOUR BIZ-NICHE	*The narrow focus of selling your product or service to a subcategory of people with low competition.*

LIZY'S WHO + WHAT + WHY

For Lizy it looked like this:

WHO	Homebuyers.
WHAT	Choose her as a loan officer.
WHY	Because she could help qualify buyers that other loan officers would pass on.
LIZY'S BIZ-NICHE	*Lizy specialized in loans that require extra steps.*

WHO

The who is the group of people to whom you are attempting to sell your service or product.

You would be shocked at how many businesses can't answer the simple question, "Who is your customer?" The answer to this question is vital, and it rarely changes, even as other elements of your business tend to shift. Oh, and here's a hint—the answer is never "everyone."

WHAT

I wanted you to purchase this book. Lizy wanted homebuyers to select her as their loan officer. What is it, specifically, that you want *your* customer to do?

You may be thinking, *Obviously, I want people to buy from me.* That may be true. But you need to be specific. Think about it, decide, then write it down. You need to see the situation as clearly as possible.

WHY

Why would anyone choose you or your business over a competitor?

Lizy's why was perfect because it didn't involve any convincing. She offered a path to homeownership that her contemporaries didn't.

~~~~~

Once you input the who, what, and why, the Biz-Niche becomes pretty clear.

Lizy needed to reach homebuyers (who), who would select her as their loan officer (what). These homebuyers would use Lizy because other loan officers wouldn't be able to get them approved, or wouldn't even try (why). So, Lizy specialized in one loan type (Biz-Niche). She didn't go after everyone; instead, she found a slim portion of the marketplace others had overlooked or were unwilling to serve. She dominated this underserved niche, which enabled her to have less competition.

There's something I don't want you to miss here—you can't fake your business with some fancy ideas. All the niching in the world won't help if you actually aren't good at delivering. If Lizy were terrible at getting difficult loan applications approved, she wouldn't have lasted long in that Biz-Niche. Only because she was good at delivering did her niche work. The same goes for DSC—only because their razors were high quality did they grow a loyal customer base that grew their company into the billions.

EVERY COMPANY CAN USE THIS FORMULA

The Biz-Niche formula works for every business regardless of industry, competition, or whether you're new or established, local or national, or selling a product or a service. Successful companies start with a Biz-Niche, and from there they often take over everything. In some cases, I mean "everything" literally, like in Amazon's case.

When most of us think of Amazon, we instinctively think of a business that, per their company's motto, sells "everything from A to Z." But Amazon started with a Biz-Niche. Originally, they only sold books to people willing to purchase online.

AMAZON'S WHO

Of course, at first, some people resisted online shopping. Most wanted to feel a product before they bought it, and giving out personal payment information online wasn't the norm. So Amazon's who was not everyone. It was limited to early internet adopters who were willing to store their credit or debit cards online to buy something without physically holding it.

AMAZON'S WHAT

In the long term, Amazon's what was to increase sales. Every business wants that. But more specifically, in the short term, Amazon wanted people to feel increasingly comfortable storing their payment information online. Convincing people to do this was difficult at first.

FOR B2B OR PARTNER-RELIANT READERS

If you're not a B2B or in a partner-reliant space, then you can skip this note.

We assumed that Lizy is trying to reach homebuyers. But Lizy could have considered her situation from a different perspective. She could have, instead, assumed that her customer (her who) was actually the *real estate agent*, and that what she needed *them* to do was recommended her to homebuyers (what). The "why" would then be because other loan officers wouldn't be able to get the real estate agent's client approved. If you look at Lizy's situation from that perspective, her Biz-Niche formula would look like this:

WHO	Real estate agents.
WHAT	Recommend her to the homebuyer.
WHY	Because she could help qualify buyers that other loan officers would pass on.
LIZY'S BIZ-NICHE	*Lizy specialized in loans that require extra steps.*

Notice that not a lot changed in this alternative perspective. Likely, you don't need to consider this alternative perspective, and if this confuses you, just forget it. But if you're in a B2B company or in an industry or business that relies heavily on a partner, you know exactly why I brought this up. Often, when finding your Biz-Niche, flipping around your "who" can help you better understand your situation.

AMAZON'S WHY

Bezos took immaculate care in nailing the why for his company. Amazon offered, and still offers, insane customer convenience, making Amazon what Bezos famously calls "the most customer-centric company" on Earth. Amazon has always relentlessly focused on ease of purchase. Perhaps the most succinct way to crystallize what Amazon offered those early adopters, and continues to offer to this day, is "extreme convenience."

AMAZON'S BIZ-NICHE

Bezos knew he wanted to focus on extreme convenience (why) and those who were willing to purchase and store their payment information online (who and what), so he did plenty of research, and landed on the book category.

So, Amazon's Biz-Niche became "selling every book online to those willing to make online purchases." Bezos nailed it.

He successfully leveraged the power of the internet to connect book buyers with their favorite tomes, allowing a guy who started in his garage to compete against established, multi-million-dollar businesses like Borders and Barnes & Noble. As Amazon's customer base grew, founded on their original Biz-Niche, customers became more comfortable making purchases online. Plus, once their information was stored on their account, it was easy for Amazon to encourage an additional purchase. This convenience enabled Amazon to expand into other product offerings until, eventually, Amazon became "the everything store."

RESPOND TO THE MARKET

Amazon self-defined their Biz-Niche. Alternatively, the marketplace may nudge you into a niche, as it did with Lizy, and Instagram.

Originally, Instagram started as an app called Burbn that allowed users to check in at various locations (similar to Foursquare). While the app was under development, it became clear to the founders that beta users really liked Burbn's photo filters, but they didn't use much else. So the founders pivoted, and niched down on photo filters, because they were responding to their customers. In fact, they doubled down on that niche so much that, originally, they only allowed users to post 1" by 1" photos and nothing else. Talk about niche!

It worked, and Instagram sold to Facebook in 2012 for $1 billion.

This listen-to-your-customers strategy that Instagram and Lizy used is effective, and so is Amazon's more proactive approach, where they chose their Biz-Niche without much input from their customer. Both can be effective strategies.

So, which strategy should you take?

The answer often lies in whether or not you already have an established business with established customers. If you do have an established business with customers, the goal isn't to change your Biz-Niche. It's to uncover exactly what it already is (which is what Burbn did). If you are already selling, you need to look at your current customers, and then double down on what's working. Alternatively, if you don't have customers yet, then start somewhere, and listen to the marketplace as you expand.

Successful companies like Amazon, Instagram, and even my wife's real estate business use the Biz-Niche formula to find and define their Biz-Niche. This helps orient your entire company's efforts. Later, you can expand.

In the next chapter, we'll walk through how you can find your own Biz-Niche, please.

SUMMARY

From new entrepreneurs to billion-dollar tech companies, successful businesses start with one Biz-Niche, providing one offering to one subcategory of people. Successful entrepreneurs must do the same. This enables them to focus on the important aspects of their business and expand through that area.

Key takeaways:

- Your Biz-Niche: the narrow focus of selling your product or service to a subcategory of people with low competition.
- Biz-Niche:
    - → **Who:** Who do you want to reach with your product or service?
    - → **+ What:** What action(s) do you want them to take?
    - → **+ Why:** Why would they choose you over the competition?

☛ Every company can use this formula. Regardless of industry or customer demographic, this formula provides a simple path to narrowing your business focus.

CHAPTER 4

Find Your Biz-Niche

Harry's a typical corporate guy. He's fifty-five, and he's worked diligently in his career for a couple decades. He likes his job, but you know what he *loves*?

Trail running.

He's been running for approximately ten years now, and here's what he's learned:

- Running a few miles a day provides him with a clear mind for his day at the office.
- He meets like-minded people out on the trail.
- Trail running keeps him in excellent shape.
- Trail-running hats suck.

That last one is a bigger deal than Harry first imagined. It's a problem all his trail-running comrades have noticed. None of their hats last long on the harsh Colorado trails. Either that, or they're bulky and create unnecessary heat, putting a drag on runs. Consequently, Harry's constantly buying new hats, then throwing them out because he can't seem to find a quality, lightweight hat to run in that doesn't hold in heat and sweat.

Finally, he decides to create his own. After all, how hard can it be? He gives it a shot by sewing together some mesh, wire, and fabric. The first few tries fall apart, but, after a couple weeks, he's made a hat that's lightweight, and it holds its shape even after stuffing it into his pockets. Also, it's breathable. Perfect.

His running friends keep asking him where he bought his hat and how they can buy one. He makes one or two and gives them away as gifts. Then he gets more requests from their friends. He makes a few more and sells them just above cost. Eventually, people well outside his immediate network are asking for them regularly. Harry starts to think, *Maybe this hat thing could be a real money-maker if I gave it enough effort?*

If Harry wants to say "bye" to his boss, he'll need to sell significantly more hats. Right now, for his limited sales, Harry is hand-making each hat. If Harry had enough sales to order a thousand hats at a time from a professional manufacturer, then he'd be able to bring the cost per hat down much lower, helping him turn a better profit.

Harry's first stop is finding his who. Harry already has customers, so he just needs to find more people like his current customers—more trail runners.

As for Harry's what, it's all about the specific action that he wants his customer to take. At this point, Harry wants people to buy his hats. Pretty simple.

Harry already knows why people will buy his product, because it's the same reason he would: there isn't another high-quality hat that works for trail runners' unique needs.

WHO	Trail runners.
WHAT	Buy his hats.
WHY	Because there isn't another quality product designed for trail runners' specific needs.
HARRY'S BIZ-NICHE	*Selling high-quality breathable hats designed for trail runners.*

I know what you may be thinking. *Skyler. I got it. This isn't rocket science.* You're right. It's not rocket science. But as your business moves forward, you'll need to refer to your Biz-Niche as your North Star to constantly align, evaluate, and filter decisions accordingly, so don't overlook it.

TYPES OF BUSINESS

Harry represents one type of business, selling a product.
You may be there. Maybe you sell, or want to sell, athleisure, stickers, remote control cars, or a new, patented toy.
If you're selling a "thing," you're selling a product. The
other type of business is selling a service. Maybe you're a
freelance writer, a CPA, or a dance choreographer. When
you boil everything down, every business is either *selling a
product* or *selling a service.*

> When you boil everything down, every business is either
> *selling a product* or *selling a service.*

Of course, some businesses do both. You can buy a washer
and dryer from Home Depot, and you can also pay them
to install the appliances in your home. In that case, they're
selling products and services.

Of course, whenever I boil business down to these two categories, the modern mind screams, *What about influencers? Where do they fit in?*

Yes, today it's possible to have an internet following based on nearly anything, from your photography skills to your niche understanding of a seemingly fringe topic, like the Teenage Mutant Ninja Turtles. Many people who create content or have niche understanding build huge audiences, and they make money off these audiences. These are what's known as "influencers," "content creators," or simply "creators." You may know some of their names: Charli D'Amelio, Julia Berelezhoeimer, Ninja, Shea Serrano, or Casey Neistat.

These individuals may seem like they're a whole new category of business. Not really—they're still selling something. If a creator is selling their content (like photographs or books), they're simply selling a product. If someone is influencing their followers to purchase someone else's product, they are still selling something. These influencers are essentially selling the *attention* from their audience. For instance, if Coca-Cola pays an influencer to take a picture of their new beverage and then make a shoutout to their 10 gazillion fans, the influencer has essentially sold attention to Coca-Cola.

This distinction may seem remedial or unimportant, but

it's worth pointing out, because businesses often forget that an audience's attention must be monetized. Without monetizing attention, you don't have a business.

SELLING A SERVICE: BIZ-NICHE FOR REALTOR RACHEL

Okay, so throughout our time together, we'll follow Harry, who's selling a product. But what about the other type of business, selling a service?

Enter Rachel, who lives in Charleston, South Carolina. She's at a major crossroads in life. She recently divorced, and she also lost her part-time real estate gig with the rest of her team when COVID-19 hit. Now, since her two teenage kids can drive, they depend on her much less, and she has the asset of time. Plus, even though she was laid off from her former employer, many of her former clients (homebuyers) want to work with her specifically. Also, most of those clients are female homebuyers who connect well with Rachel because she's similar to them; she's recently single, and she's open with clients about the struggles of single parenthood.

Rachel's target customer is constricted to a geography (i.e., Charleston). That's normal for many businesses that are selling a service. Also, female customers are particularly attracted to Rachel's personality and openness. That all goes into her who.

Rachel wants people to select her as their real estate agent; that's her what.

Those who choose Rachel select her because she understands their perspective as single moms. Rachel will use this reasoning as her why. Will doubling down on this mean losing other customers? Perhaps, but she'll probably only lose those who weren't likely to be good clients and appreciate her services anyway. By honing her why, she is likely to attract more of the right customers.

Here's how Rachel's Biz-Niche breaks down:

WHO	Female homebuyers in Charleston, South Carolina.
WHAT	Use her as their real estate agent.
WHY	Because she connects well with them, building trust and long-term relationships.
RACHEL'S BIZ-NICHE	*Selling homes to female homebuyers in Charleston, South Carolina.*

Rachel can now focus all her mental energy and efforts on a specific homebuyer with a specific psychology in a specific location. (Normally, I would tell someone in Rachel's position to narrow down to a specific price range of homes, but for the purposes of this book, we'll leave that aside.)

WHAT'S YOUR BIZ-NICHE?

So you get the idea. Now, it's your turn to fill in your who, what, and why, to find your Biz-Niche. Getting this on paper will help you. And you can write in this book, because you paid for it, and your elementary school teacher will never know.

At the end of this book, I'll have a new page where you can write down all three of your niches together. You can download additional blank copies at SkylerIrvine.com/nicheplease.

WHO	Who do you want to reach with your product or service?
WHAT	What action(s) do you want them to take?
WHY	Why would they choose you over the competition?
YOUR BIZ-NICHE	*The narrow focus of selling your product or service to a subcategory of people with low competition.*

As you're filling this out, keep these tips in mind:

KNOW WHEN TO PIVOT

You will pivot.

The Biz-Niche is not a one-and-done. You aren't going to be doing exactly one thing forever. In fact, that sort of thinking is exactly why businesses fail. You want to be open to continuous innovation and constant pivoting. Think about Netflix.

When Netflix first launched, Blockbuster was king of the movie rental business. They had rental stores everywhere. But Netflix launched as a new company solving the biggest issue people had with Blockbuster—returning movies on time.

At the time, Blockbuster wasn't running their business with their customer, their who, in mind. Instead, they were running their business based on a revenue model that charged excessive late fees. Customers hated it. Late fees typically cost more than the movie rentals themselves, which is exactly what Blockbuster was counting on, and Blockbuster became addicted to this revenue stream.

But when a business attaches itself to a particular revenue stream, instead of attaching itself to their customer, they leave themselves vulnerable to disruption.

Netflix pounced on Blockbuster's oversight. They aggressively pitched that customers could order movies online and return them whenever they wanted and therefore would never have to pay a late fee. By the time Blockbuster realized what was happening to their customer base, it was too late. They had failed to pivot in time, and they rapidly became obsolete, giving way to the new era of at-home movie consumption.

But Netflix didn't sit on their success. While they originally enjoyed a prosperous revenue stream built upon the no-late-fees model, they didn't grow addicted to it. After taking down Blockbuster, they kept iterating to focus even more on their who. They moved online, pivoting to streaming people's favorite content online from a variety of outside content sources, like Disney and popular TV shows. This worked well, as people wanted to watch their favorite movies and shows on-demand, again and again. Netflix quickly expanded to millions of users.

But Netflix still didn't become addicted. They pivoted again. Instead of just finding everyone's favorite TV shows and movies from outside studios, Netflix began to make their own quality content in-house. Now, they've won Emmy awards for their shows, won Oscars for their movies, and attracted A-list directors, producers, and actors to their studio. They did so well at the Oscars, Spielberg wanted the rules changed so that Netflix movies couldn't compete. (If Spielberg thinks you're stiff competition, you've made it.) That's what happens when you constantly stay focused on your customer and are willing to pivot as often and frequently as necessary.

By 2020, various news outlets reported that Netflix had passed the 200-million-subscriber mark; Blockbuster, on the other hand, had one remaining store in Bend, Oregon, which has mainly served as a novelty shop of a time mostly forgotten.

Be like Netflix, not Blockbuster, and know when to pivot.

GIVING (VALUE) IS BETTER THAN RECEIVING

Other than refusing to pivot, another reason once-successful companies fail is because they focus more on extracting value rather than giving it.

In 1975, an engineer at Eastman Kodak invented a self-contained electronic photographic device. In simpler terms, the engineer had created the world's first known digital camera. Executives of Kodak shut down the project. They feared this new invention would impact their top revenue-maker, photo film sales. Like Blockbuster, Kodak wasn't focused on their current customers; they focused on their current revenue stream.

In 2012, Kodak filed for bankruptcy.

In both cases, Kodak's and Blockbuster's short-term greed created long-term losses. This is unfortunately common. Companies fail when they try to extract value from their customers rather than looking for new, creative ways to *provide* value. That's why Kodak missed the opportunity to lead with digital photography. Conversely, smart companies constantly think, *How can we improve our customer experience? How can we offer more value?* In the long term, customers usually reward these companies.

THE INTERNET IS THE GREAT EQUALIZER

There's another thing you should keep in mind when constructing your Biz-Niche. Ask yourself this question: *what do Netflix, Amazon, and other, modern successful businesses have in common?*

I'll give you a hint. They all leverage the internet.

Bezos would have had a hard time beating Barnes & Noble without it, as physical bookstores can't possibly hold every available book. Instead, Bezos brokered deals with enough bookstores to provide a one-stop shop for every book, without having to hold all of them himself. That was only efficiently possible with the internet. The same is true with Netflix. Their current streaming platform would be impossible without widespread internet access. Even their earlier DVD-by-mail model was built using the internet, as it heavily relied on customers making video selections online.

The power of the internet gives the small business with the excellent idea the opportunity to jump over, or completely avoid, roadblocks that bigger players have counted on for decades.

> The power of the internet gives the small business with the excellent idea the opportunity to jump over, or completely avoid, roadblocks that bigger players have counted on for decades.

Until the internet paved the way for disruption, Blockbuster, Barnes & Noble, and others successfully leveraged their size to keep smaller players from having a seat at the table. But now, no one can stop the small players. You or I can start a business in a living room and have global exposure with the click of a button, without expensive TV ads. Someone can create content with their iPhone and put it online for millions to see, without having to own a movie theater. Another individual can gather customer testimonials and reviews without ever getting out of bed.

Simply put, the internet is the great equalizer. It's helped plenty of small businesses and entrepreneurs who were thinking, *I need to supercharge my niche, please!*

SUMMARY

Every business can use the Biz-Niche formula to narrow their focus onto the most effective business plan. There are two types of businesses. Ultimately, every business is either selling a product or selling a service.

- Harry's Biz-Niche is selling high-quality breathable hats designed for trail runners. We'll follow him through this book to provide an example of finding all three of your niches if you are selling a product.
- Rachel's Biz-Niche is selling homes to female home-buyers in Charleston, South Carolina. We'll follow her through this book to provide an example of finding all three of your niches if you are selling a service.
- Know when to pivot. Businesses throughout history have failed because they arrived at their Biz-Niche and never reiterated themselves.
- Giving value is better than receiving. Successful companies consistently think of providing value to their

customers. They focus on their who, not on creating short-term profits. In the end, customers often reward the business.

- The internet is the great equalizer. The internet has created a level playing field, allowing small businesses to compete in industries that were previously dominated by clunky, outdated businesses that took advantage of complex ecosystems.

Part III

Your Content Niche

CHAPTER 5

The Most Important, Shortest Chapter

In the next part, Your Content Niche, we're going to help you find a type of content that is best for your business, like a blog or a podcast that has a specific target in mind. In the next few chapters, you'll probably find skills you didn't know you had, and we'll take a deeper look at you, your business, your customer, and the competition. We'll combine all those ingredients together and find a Content Niche that is perfect for you—one that you actually enjoy using.

If creating content sounds overwhelming, don't worry. I know how you feel, because I've seen it dozens of times from business owners and entrepreneurs who come into my office. I help guide them through the whole maze, and by the end, they're relieved.

Honestly, finding a Content Niche is pretty easy. First, get yourself a beer, a cup of your favorite tea or coffee, or a glass of infused water. After you're relaxed, read the next few chapters with an open mind to find your second niche, please.

CHAPTER 6

The Content Niche Equation

For a long time, only an exclusive group discussed wine, and they did it with reverence.

Wine snobs donned bow ties and long dresses. They stroked their wannabe French moustaches or manicures as they sniffed, sipped, and slowly swirled an ounce of an expensive juice just before declaring something about it tasting "angular" or having "high tannin levels." With sophisticated taste and complicated terminology, wine elitists danced with an air of superiority above the mediocrity of the common man.

That is until along came GaryVee.

In 2006, GaryVee made a bold move. He created an online,

daily wine show called *Wine Library TV*. He had already helped expand his family liquor business, so he knew as much about wine as any reverent connoisseur. But GaryVee is anything but reverent.

As he critiqued different wine selections on his online video series, GaryVee dropped f-bombs, talked about his favorite sports team (the New York Jets), and even compared wine nuances to breakfast cereals. He was nothing like the traditional wine aficionados, and he never tried to be. Instead, he made wine accessible to the common man by being himself, a common man.

GaryVee's content wasn't successful.

It was explosive.

And that early wine show started a chain of smart content moves by GaryVee, who eventually opened his own media company called VaynerMedia (among other businesses). Today, he's worth about $160 million, and it all started with a daily online video series about wine.

Be like GaryVee.

~~~~~

What exactly was it that made GaryVee successful?

Simply put, he found a Content Niche, a type of content that was easy and fun for him to consistently produce. GaryVee's original Content Niche was a daily online video series about wine that included tons of personality. Once GaryVee found that Content Niche, he began to double down and create content like crazy, which propelled him into international business fame.

While we don't all need to be GaryVee, we can borrow from his lessons. His story illuminates a pathway to successfully creating exciting and fun social media content.

If you're a small-business owner or an entrepreneur, you need to copy GaryVee's model and find a specific content that is easy and fun for you to consistently produce, so that you can build a dedicated following on social media who will buy from you.

You *could* try to create a thousand different types of content, from videos to blogs to tweets to pictures, but if you do that, I can tell you the outcome:

You'll get burned out. Quickly.

Instead, you should find *one* type of content to consistently create, and then from there, turn followers into customers. Later down the road, you can expand and make various types of content, if necessary. But just as creating a Biz-

Niche is crucial to keeping your business offerings efforts focused, so is creating a Content Niche crucial to keeping your content focused.

~~~~~

To be clear, when we talk about your Content Niche, we are *not* talking about the platforms themselves, such as Instagram, Facebook, or Twitter. All of the specific platforms will be discussed later, in Part IV: Your Media Niche. For now, we are talking about the content *type*. A podcast directed at single dads, a video series made for technology experts, and a photography series aimed at senior citizens are all Content Niches. Conversely, TikTok, LinkedIn, and YouTube are all Media Niches.

So, how do you find your Content Niche? Let's look at Gary-Vee's *Wine Library TV* story.

Notice that GaryVee did not start by creating a gazillion different types of content. Instead, he originally doubled down on one area that became wildly successful. And he didn't just get lucky by choosing an online video series about wine for less-than-reverent wine drinkers. He purposely, thoughtfully crafted his own Content Niche.

First, he thought about himself, his own personality, his superpowers, what he loves, what he hates, and all his idiosyncrasies. Crucially, GaryVee's rambunctious personality is one people like to see and experience within a media-rich environment.

Second, he considered what content makes sense for his business, selling wine. Wine is nice to look at, it doesn't have any audio qualities, and it's all about the taste.

Third, he considered his customer. He wasn't going after traditional wine connoisseurs. Instead, he was pursuing the hipper, probably younger, wine drinker, who was willing to stray from the traditionalism of the elite wine connoisseurs. Also, GaryVee correctly assumed these hipper, younger drinkers were likely to be more tech-savvy than their traditional counterparts.

Lastly, GaryVee considered his competition. He asked himself, *What is my competition not doing?*

Put it all together, and GaryVee's mental process follows an equation we can all use. I call it the Content Niche equation. For GaryVee, it looked something like this:

GARY	GaryVee is loud, fun, irreverent.
GARY'S BUSINESS	GaryVee's business is selling what could be a visual product that people will ultimately taste and smell.
GARY'S CUSTOMER	Nontraditional wine drinkers, who are probably young, hip, and tech-savvy.
MINUS THE COMPETITION	Most wine companies weren't focused on making content.
GARY'S CONTENT NICHE	*A daily online video series about wine.*

All of us can follow a similar path.

If we generalize the above box, it looks like this:

YOU	What skills, experiences, and natural advantages do you have, and what are your interests, passions, hobbies, personality traits, quirks, etc.?
YOUR BUSINESS	What makes your business unique? Also, does your business lend itself to a particular sensory experience? For example, are you selling something that must be seen, worn, heard, or tasted?
YOUR CUSTOMER	What are the demographics of your customer? (Do they come from a particular age group, are they male or female, are they located within a specific region, what's their income level, etc.)
MINUS THE COMPETITION	Subtract the type of content that your competition is already making.
YOUR CONTENT NICHE	*The specific type of content you create, based on you, your business, your customer, minus the competition.*

So let's break down every area of the equation. We'll start with the part everyone likes the most:

You.

YOU

While no one can ever be GaryVee, you can take this away from GaryVee's story: be you, with all your quirks and passions. Maybe you like to draw, maybe you like to paint. Or, maybe you're really interested in nature. Perhaps you're quiet, introverted, and contemplative, or maybe you're loud, boisterous, and extraverted. All of those things, whether related to your business or not, are part of you, and all of them go into your Content Niche.

Just like with GaryVee's quirky personality, all your "you-isms" combine to create something unmistakably individual that no one can copy. I call all these superpowers, and it's like having a free patent for life. Everyone has these superpowers, but so often they go untapped. Some people overlook or underuse them, while others are even embarrassed by them. Oddly, that embarrassment is pretty normal—even real superheroes have had that problem.

If you've ever seen a superhero origin movie, you'll notice something odd. The hero almost never recognizes their special abilities as superpowers. Usually, they try to cover them up because they don't know how to use them effectively. People make this same mistake when it comes to their own superpowers. They mistake what they have as not valuable, or they subconsciously believe that making a living should be a drudgery, so they bury their superpowers, or relegate them to hobbies. For instance, photography becomes a side thing a gifted photographer only does on weekends, when they could be using it to market their construction business. Or a fantastic storyteller only shows off their storytelling abilities at family get-togethers, instead of applying that strength to their clothing business they've always wanted to start.

That doesn't have to be you.

Just as the superheroes learn in the movies, you don't have to completely toss your superpower. You just need to learn to wield it, so you don't blow anything up.

I can't promise that your superpowers will make you Cyclops, but I can promise that you'll feel like you buried your superpowers if you never learn to use them.

That's one thing I love about doing what I do—I get to help people rediscover their superpowers, and help them learn to effectively use them, just like in the movies: The superhero always learns how to use their superpowers. Only, you probably can't fly, and I'm definitely not Professor X.

YOUR BUSINESS

Your business is important because, often, the type of business you have lends itself to a type of content. For instance, if you sell accounting services, people are likely interested in reading some charts and examples of what you do. Whereas, if you sell a highly visual product such as dresses, people are probably more interested in seeing pictures or videos of someone wearing them.

GaryVee sold wines, which are nice to look at. Consider your own business in the same way: Do you sell something that is highly visual? Is it something that customers purchase once or often? Is it expensive? Does it go on a shelf, in the driveway, or in a home?

Also, in this part of the equation, you want to consider what you love about your business. Do you love working with your customers? Do you love the actual product or service you provide? Are you passionate about vendor or partner relationships? Do you love solving problems? Is your company culture the most important thing to you?

YOUR CUSTOMER

We've talked about you and your business. Now, let's talk about your customer. You need to know who is most likely to say yes to your business. This is similar to the who from the Biz-Niche, but now we are taking it one layer deeper.

Here, you want to define your customer as narrowly as realistically possible. I put together a few questions to get you started, but there may be other data that is more pertinent to your business, product or service, or industry.

- Do your customers come from a particular age group?
- Are they male or female or both?
- Do they come from a certain geography?
- Do they make a certain income level?

There are many other questions you could ask, but these should get you started. Keep digging, and you'll see patterns emerge.

MINUS COMPETITION

Once you put in everything about you, your business, and your customer, you're left with just one element: the competition. I save that one for last, because it acts as a conclusion to what you're really doing with your Content Niche.

When you're looking for a Content Niche, you're essentially asking what content you can create for your customer in a way few, or none, of your competitors has. GaryVee did a daily video series, partially because it made sense for him, his business, his customer, but also because his competition wasn't doing a daily video series.

Too often, entrepreneurs take the opposite route, and look to their competition for guidance. But typically, you don't want to create the exact same content as all your competitors. That's like trying to catch up with a race car driver by driving exactly like them at the same speed, but several laps behind. If they're already in front of you, you can't take their turns and drive at their speed, because that only guarantees that you'll never catch them, let alone pass them. You must have a different approach.

So, after you put in you, your business, your customer, don't forget to take out what's already being done. Because, in the end, you must find your own niche, please.

SUMMARY

A Content Niche is highly customized to your unique personality, customer, and business, and strays from what's been done by competitors. To gain attention from your customers, you need to find a Content Niche that you enjoy creating consistently. Entrepreneurs who spread their efforts thin on a variety of content find themselves disillusioned, inconsistently creating a variety of content, with no results.

Key takeaways:

- You have unique superpowers. Recognizing these superpowers is the first part of finding your Content Niche. Often, we don't know or recognize our superpowers. However, a lifetime of unique experiences and lessons affords each individual particular skills and talents that cannot be replicated. When you point these toward the marketplace, an explosion happens. Okay, not a real explosion. But you get the idea.
- Your Content Niche is the specific type of content you create, based on you, your business, your customer, minus the competition.

📢 Content Niche:

→ **You:** What skills, experiences, and natural advantages do you have, and what are your interests, passions, hobbies, personality traits, quirks, etc.?

→ **+ Your Business:** What makes your business unique? Also, does your business lend itself to a particular sensory experience? For example, are you selling something that must be seen, worn, heard, or tasted?

→ **+ Your Customer:** What are the demographics of your customer? (Do they come from a particular age group, are they male or female, are they located within a specific region, what's their income level, etc.)

→ **- The Competition:** Subtract the type of content that your competition is already making.

CHAPTER 7

A Crash Course in Marketing

Once upon a time, a guy decided to sell premium hot dogs. He relished over every element—the temperature of the buns, the two pickles he put on each dog, and the home-made ketchup he drizzled on top.

But not everyone was willing to pay for such a delicacy. Quickly, he figured out that the only people willing to pay for his expensive hot dogs were football fans. So, his simple Biz-Niche became selling premium hot dogs to football fans.

Next up, he needed to do some marketing. Hot dog guy is pretty smart. He didn't market to everyone: he didn't create podcasts for vegetarians, make Instagram posts directed at badminton fans, or bother with producing TV commercials for HGTV.

You see, hot dog guy knew that he only needed to market his hot dogs to one group of people:

Football fans.

Think like a hot dog guy.

~~~~~

Before we go any further with your Content Niche, we need to do a crash course in marketing. I'm going to save you the headache of reading a ton of books, listening to a million podcasts, or getting an MBA. And you aren't cheating yourself by taking my crash course, because marketing is simple.

As we discussed in Chapter 2 when we talked about soap operas, marketing is all about attention. A business could seek attention by putting an ad on television, posting pictures on Instagram, talking about their services on the radio, or paying a teenager to stand on the side of the road and jump up and down in a chicken suit. All of those efforts are seeking attention, and, by definition, marketing.

Most small businesses and entrepreneurs, if they do any marketing at all, go about it in a haphazard fashion. Maybe they throw up some flyers around town, post a few times on several different social media websites, or even buy some advertisement space on a bus stop bench. In the end, they've spread their efforts thin, spent tons of money, and have very little to show for it.

That's where smart marketing comes in.

Marketing seeks attention.

Smart marketing seeks attention from people who are likely to say yes, using the easiest possible method.

> Marketing seeks attention.
>
> *Smart* marketing seeks attention from people who are likely to say yes, using the easiest possible method.

It wouldn't do Harry the hat guy much good to market his trail-running hats to ballerinas or Rachel the real estate agent much good to market herself in a city where she isn't licensed to sell real estate. Harry needs attention from trail runners, and Rachel needs attention from female home-buyers in Charleston.

Congratulations, you've completed the first phase in my crash course on marketing. You get an A+.

THE FOUR WAYS TO GAIN ATTENTION

Now, there is something you do need to know about marketing and seeking attention. You need to know how attention works.

Attention is especially important for new businesses to understand. While an established company may be able to survive based on their brand recognition, a new business must know how to gain new attention if they wish to thrive. It's a bit like the new kid versus the popular kid in school. Everyone always seems to know about the popular kid's birthday party, even without an invite. So, the popular kid has lots of friends show up to their party. But for the new kid in school, no one knows about them or their party. The new kid must know how to get everyone's attention to invite others to their birthday party.

If you're reading this book, you're probably the "new kid" in business. So, it pays to understand attention.

Primarily, there are four main types of content that you can use to gain your customer's attention:

- Written word
- Audio
- Video
- Images

No matter what Content Niche you end up with, it will primarily fall into one of these four main categories.

Understanding these four main categories of content will help you choose your own Content Niche in Chapter 8. As you read over the next several pages, you'll find examples of individuals who selected a Content Niche within one of these categories and dominated. I'll also offer pros and cons for each category. Importantly, whatever content you create could be a mixture of two or even all four of these content types. It's just important to understand the foundational pillars of the written word, audio, video, and images.

The written word in particular is foundational to most other forms of marketing, and it's almost impossible to create any type of content without writing something, somewhere in the process. Which is exactly why we will start phase two of our crash course on marketing with the written word.

And there's no one who understands the written word better than Josh Brown.

CONTENT TYPE I: WRITTEN WORD

A couple decades ago, the financial sector was a tight-lipped community. You didn't write books giving financial advice, unless you were Secretary of the Treasury or your name was Buffett. Plus, the few financial books that were available discussed financial theory and other sophisticated topics that were broadly inaccessible and impractical for the non-academic. Starting an online blog for the "common folk" to understand "complicated financial matters" would have been laughed at.

Until Josh Brown.

"Downtown" Josh Brown broke all the rules. He was an industry insider who worked on Wall Street, and he wanted to open up the once-tight-lipped financial community and share his insider information with the world. So, what did he do? He started tweeting financial advice. I'm sure he turned some heads with elitist financiers, but Josh Brown's audience loved it.

And his audience still loves it.

Josh Brown is now the co-founder and CEO of Ritholtz Wealth Management, an author of multiple best-selling financial books, and a regular contributor on CNBC, and he even appeared on an episode of Showtime's *Billions*. In 2013, *The Wall Street Journal* ranked him as the number-one financial follow on Twitter. Of course Josh Brown ranked as number one in that category—he invented it.

He did everything you aren't supposed to do in his industry. It wasn't the norm for experts to give written financial advice, especially for free and online. However, Brown saw an opportunity. He stayed authentic to his expertise (the financial industry) and his unique superpower (writing) while considering his audience and seizing the marketing opportunity afforded by the Twitter platform.

Be like Josh Brown.

WRITTEN WORD: BASICS

Written word is the most overlooked aspect of social media. It covers long-form writing, such as email, newsletters, blog posts, news articles, books, Facebook posts, and Wikipedia. There is also short-form writing, such as print ads; "microblogging," such as tweets; and copywriting.

One of the great benefits of pursuing attention through the written word is that you need very little equipment to start. Starting a blog is free through services like Blogger or WordPress, and, even if you don't own a computer, you could go to your public library and use one, for free. While writing can be difficult, unsexy, and tedious, it has the lowest barriers to entry. Still, while starting is easy, mastering this art form can take a lifetime.

WRITTEN WORD: HOW TECH CAN HELP

There are a variety of ways that tech can help grow your reach if you decide to write. For one, you can now use various technologies like speech-to-text or AI transcription to create rough first drafts of writing without actually having to manually type anything. Also, services like Rev can create transcriptions from podcasts and video.

Also, you've probably heard of ghostwriting, when someone essentially writes a book or blog for you based on your thoughts. Celebrities, politicians, and other famous people have used ghostwriters for decades. Today, there are companies that offer streamlined ghostwriting processes to business leaders.

You can write from almost anywhere. If you're a passenger on a plane, waiting in the doctor's office, or taking a lunch break, you can write. You've probably heard of *50 Shades of Grey*. Guess what? The author, E. L. James, did much of the work on her Blackberry while riding the train to and from work.

Lastly, you can quickly publish writing, which allows you to test the marketplace. Meanwhile, other content types take much more time and resources, and often require more equipment. Therefore, writing is a great place to start because it allows you to gauge what topics resonate with your customer without having to spend much time or many resources. For instance, with Twitter or status updates, you could quickly and easily post dozens of ideas or topics in a day, see which ones resonate with your customer, and then create additional pieces of content from those posts.

WRITTEN WORD: PROS AND CONS

The written word requires you to have someone's full attention, especially if it's long form (like a book). That's a pro, but it's also a con. Because for someone to give you their full attention, they must actually be able to set aside their full attention. I don't need to explain the increasingly difficult challenge that poses in today's society. Content like microblogging and status updates on LinkedIn and Facebook are combating this issue by requiring full attention for less time.

Another pro and con of the written word is that it gives audiences the power to implement their own imagination. When people read, they are often filtering the written word through whatever happened in their day, for better or worse.

On the plus side, there is something nostalgic and romantic about the idea of regularly curling up with a book and a cup of coffee in the evening or reading the Sunday paper at the breakfast table. The written word can become a romantic, regularized pastime, which is a huge plus for marketers.

A potential negative is that it's difficult to build a personal connection through reading. Readers can't see the face or hear the voice of the author.

Lastly, another potential downside is that some people hate reading. Plus, most learning disabilities, like dyslexia, disproportionately impact the written word.

BASEBALL CARD FOR THE WRITTEN WORD

CONSIDER THIS IF...	Obviously, if you love to write, written word may be best for you.
MY BOLD PREDICTION	As attention spans get shorter and shorter, fewer and fewer people read. But that's little more than an observation. My bold prediction is that because fewer people are reading, fewer people will be writing quality books, leaving only a few good writers. When the attention pendulum swings back and content consumers start demanding long-form books again, the remaining writers will be ready to take *all* the attention.
WHY I LOVE THIS	Writing is essential for life, not just marketing. Learning to write well will help with resumes, professional emails, and even love letters. No time is ever wasted developing this skill.
HOW TO REPURPOSE	While you want to pick only one Content Niche for now, eventually you may want to branch out into other content types. When it's time to branch out with your content efforts, there's usually a natural next step to easily repurpose your content. For example, YouTube video can easily be turned into podcasts, and a collection of blogs can easily be turned into a book. Written word, in particular, is the foundational content type for much of marketing.
	From the written word, the next easiest category to branch into is audio content.
WHO'S CRUSHING IT	Here are a few people to explore who are crushing it with holding attention through the written word:
	David Perell (Twitter: @david_perell)
	Taylor Lorenz (Twitter: @TaylorLorenz)
	Amanda Goetz (Twitter: @AmandaMGoetz)
	Brianne Fleming (Twitter: @brianne2k)
	Shea Serrano (Twitter: @SheaSerrano)
	Seth Godin (Twitter: @thisissethsblog)
	Polina Marinova (Twitter: @polina_marinova)

CONTENT TYPE II: AUDIO

You may already know who Malcolm Gladwell is. His first five books were all on *The New York Times* bestseller list. But after writing and selling millions of books, Gladwell realized something: Most of his audience wasn't "reading" his material. They were *listening*, via audiobooks.

This got Gladwell thinking. *If people are listening to my work instead of reading it, perhaps I should create audio content?*

So Gladwell co-founded a podcast-first media company called Pushkin Industries. One of their flagship podcasts, *Revisionist History*, is hosted by none other than Gladwell himself.

According to an article published by *The New York Times* in 2019, individual episodes of *Revisionist History*'s five seasons were downloaded up to three million times. *That's* why a best-selling author would pivot from the written word to audio.

Be like Malcolm Gladwell.

AUDIO: THE BASICS

Audio has the advantage that it happens passively, plus it usually attaches itself to another daily habit, such as going to the gym, commuting to work, or riding the subway.

Audio covers everything that we listen to. However, for our purposes, we'll focus on podcasting and audiobooks.

A major subgenre of audio, podcasting, has gained momentum at an unprecedented pace. Spotify, which already owned ears through music, has quadrupled down on podcasting the last few years. While I was creating this book, the world found out that Joe Rogan, who hosts one of the most popular podcasts, signed an exclusive deal with Spotify for approximately $100 million. While that sounds exorbitant, by the end of 2021, Spotify will have spent six times that amount buying up shows, media companies, and platforms in an effort to become the YouTube of podcasting. They're well on their way to that goal.

Audiobooks have also taken on a life of their own. In a 2017 survey, the Audiobook Publishers Association reported that almost half of all audiobook listeners were under thirty-five, which is a key indicator on how future generations will be tuning in.

INTERVIEW-BASED PODCASTING

Have you ever considered hosting an interview-based podcast show? It's not as hard as it sounds, and it gives you the perfect opportunity to connect with your *guests*, not just your listeners.

Here's how to set it up: start a podcast that is directed toward your potential customers, and then invite your customers as guests on your show so you can interview and ask them questions. You'll build relationships with the exact people you want to sell to, and you never need to ask for fifteen minutes of anyone's time. Plus, interestingly, people are likely to say yes when you ask them to come on a podcast show for an interview; it's fun to be interviewed, and it isn't nearly as intimidating as being on camera.

Plus, on a podcast, you get to ask your guests anything. So when you invite future customers on your show, it's like free market research. As long as you show genuine interest, ask thoughtful questions, and stay engaged, your guests will answer almost any question. This leads to new information for your business and helps produce the most exciting content for your listeners. As an added bonus, hosting a podcast gives you a ton of credibility, akin to authoring your own book.

AUDIO: HOW TECH CAN HELP

Technology has revolutionized the audio world. Previously, for any sort of audio consumption, people bought a physical product, such as a CD. Now, nearly anyone can download an entire audiobook or podcast straight to their handheld device. Plus, it's just as easy to record. Apps like Anchor make it easy, simple, and free to create your own podcast within seconds and make it globally available. And you can always upgrade: It's easy to start with these inexpensive (or free) products, and, after ten episodes, if podcasting proves to be a good fit for you and your business, you can invest in fancier equipment, like a professional microphone. (But honestly, you don't need to do that until after you have some episodes recorded and published.)

AUDIO: PROS AND CONS

Audio doesn't require someone's full attention, which is both a pro and a con. An audience can easily tune into a podcast or audiobook while performing another activity, so there's more time available for listening, but that time is of less quality, because attention is divided.

Another pro and con of audio is that it attaches itself to other habits. As people take the same morning drive, hop on the same treadmill, or walk their dog along the same paths, they grow accustomed to listening to a podcast or audiobook. This is usually a pro for marketers, but as COVID-19 taught us, this can also be a negative. Everyone thought podcasting was going to skyrocket as people were asked to stay in their homes in 2020. The reverse happened. Since most people listen to podcasts on their way to and from work, podcasting actually decreased without the other piece of the routine attached.

Lastly, audio also has a low barrier to entry. Although the

written word is probably the easiest attention to start with, audio is a close second. You can start hosting your very own podcast for free with just a button tap on your smartphone. When it's time to upgrade to a better microphone, you can get one for less than a hundred bucks.

BASEBALL CARD FOR AUDIO

CONSIDER THIS IF...	Many entrepreneurs may already be really good at talking. If that's you, then consider going after your customer's attention with a podcast!
MY BOLD PREDICTION	Hearables: In the near future, keep your ear out for amazing new devices that you wear like earbuds. These devices will make audio transactions, such as translation and hearing assistance, seamless and cost-effective.
WHY I LOVE THIS	Using podcasting, it takes very little time to create high-quality content and deliver it to your customer.
HOW TO REPURPOSE	You can easily repurpose audio content into video content. If you're already recording audio, it's pretty easy to turn the cameras on, and then hit "publish to YouTube." We'll discuss the video next!
WHO'S CRUSHING IT	*Animal Spirits* podcast Chelsea Peitz (*The Voice of Social Sales*) Tim Ferriss (*The Tim Ferriss Show*) Bill Simmons (*The Bill Simmons Podcast*)

CONTENT TYPE III: VIDEO

"I nominate Matt Damon for the ALS Ice Bucket Challenge!"

In the summer of 2014, a somewhat obscure disease started making headlines across America. It seemed every person in the country was suddenly nominated to dump freezing cold water over their heads and donate money to research a disease that only months ago many people couldn't accurately describe. Celebrities (like Matt Damon), politicians from both sides of the aisle, opposing athletes, moms, dads, teenagers...no one escaped nomination. And you didn't want to escape it, because you wanted to be part of the fun!

Within months, people had watched millions of videos of people dumping buckets of ice on themselves, and the ALS foundation enjoyed a hefty surge in donation dollars.

That's the power of video—in the modern era, it brings us all together, and connects us even when we are separated by thousands of miles, opposing teams, or layers of ideology.

VIDEO: THE BASICS

Creating and watching video is entirely different than creating and watching photography and design media, both of which are covered by images, which we'll discuss next.

Of all the ways to grab someone's attention, videography has undergone the most technological changes. Broader access to fast internet coupled with massive reliance on smartphones has created a world where immediate video access lives inside our pockets. The rapid pace of innovation has also put downward pressure on the cost of technology. What we can do today with video was nearly unimaginable just a decade ago. For instance, shooting aerial footage in the early 2010s was financially out of reach for 99 percent of everyday people, and most businesses. Now, for less than $1,000, anyone can purchase a drone that will deliver high-definition footage.

Filming oneself has also become commonplace. We now have two generations that have grown up with parents constantly filming them: the millennial and Gen Z generations. Across the globe, people now use Facebook Live, Instagram, and other platforms to create product reviews, "unboxings," makeup tutorials, car fixes, you name it. And that brings me to the one platform that can't be ignored when discussing video: YouTube.

YouTube was created in 2005 by PayPal ex-employees as an online video dating platform, which they even launched on Valentine's Day. Users flocked to the platform to freely share video about everything from their little brother wiping out on a skateboard to clips of their favorite TV shows.

Most enterprises wanted nothing to do with YouTube because they were terrified of the potential copyright liabilities they assumed the new platform would invite. So Google swooped in, apparently unafraid of the possible litigation, with billions of dollars. According to a *New York Times* article, Google announced their intent to purchase the platform for roughly $1.65 billion in 2006, less than two years after YouTube was founded. Now, almost five billion videos are watched on YouTube every day, and three hundred hours of video are uploaded every minute.

Of course, YouTube is just one story. There's Vimeo, Dailymotion, Facebook Live, Snapchat, Instagram video, TikTok, and others. All this points to one conclusion: people are watching video. For marketers, it can't be ignored. Not every company needs to be involved with video, especially at first, but they ought to at least understand it.

(Of course, this category does not only include online video, but also movies, TV, and animated films. Yet, for the purposes of our discussion, I assume you aren't looking to create the next Avengers movie or produce *Land Before Time 27*, so we'll focus on video shared over social media.)

Any Business Can Use Video

Not every business should use video, but every business can; whatever industry or business you're a part of, someone probably wants and needs information you have.

Whether you are using video to show customers how to use your product or service, or simply documenting how your business operates, someone will find what you're doing interesting and helpful to watch. Even if you believe your industry is uninteresting to most people, it will still be interesting to others in the same profession.

So many people and businesses are latching onto video, which is why you should keep in mind that it won't always be as powerful as it is now. The laws of supply and demand apply to attention. In the 2020s, people can't seem to get enough of video. As more and more businesses create video, the market will become saturated. Eventually, it will be so full that video will lack its novel potency, and another content will rise to power, until the supply of that content surpasses demand, and people will move, and so on.

VIDEO: HOW TECH CAN HELP

Most people make the major mistake of focusing on production quality, particularly when it comes to video. Being "on camera" carries a sort of romanticism and too often encourages perfectionism. As a media company, I've seen this firsthand. When I meet up with a client and tell them we are going to film, usually they will say something like, "I didn't know I was going to be on camera today. I need to change my clothes and put myself together."

I must often remind my clients that they meet clients and other professionals all day, dressed as they normally would, and showing those same people a video isn't any different. The entire point of producing video is to connect with customers on a personal level; people want to see what others look like after sitting in traffic and driving to meetings.

This is a hard concept for many to understand, because "back in the day" being on camera was a rare occurrence that required hours of preparation and expensive equipment. Now, cameras live in pockets and can be turned on at any moment.

Likewise, don't spend money on expensive equipment; just use your smartphone to record video. Production quality is not the most important thing. It's not even the second most important thing. First, the message of your content—what you are actually communicating to your customer—is the most important aspect of any content. Next, your focus should be on consistency. Videos are now so easy and cheap to produce, everyone's doing it. Those companies who will win in the long run are those who stay focused and consistently post.

VIDEO: PROS AND CONS

When someone is watching you, you have their full attention, and you silence outside distractions. This provides plusses and minuses. The more attention you have, the better, but the more attention you require, the harder it is to get.

Video is easy to repurpose. When you create video, you are also creating other visual and audio content, which can be easily repurposed into sound bites, podcasts, and photography. You can even turn excellent quotes into short-form writing, like microblogs or tweets.

A con of video is that there is stiff competition. Businesses and everyday people are after attention this way. Nearly every social media platform is adding some sort of video functionality, because everyone realizes its benefits.

BASEBALL CARD FOR VIDEO

CONSIDER THIS IF...	If you really like being the center of attention, then you may have found your home with video.
MY BOLD PREDICTION	In the coming future, I see virtual reality (VR) and augmented reality (AR) becoming game changers for video. For instance, you and I will eventually be able to watch the Super Bowl from the quarterback's perspective!
WHY I LOVE THIS	One video can have a tremendous impact on your business (and society) in a short time. This can be both a positive and a negative. Consider your videos wisely.
HOW TO REPURPOSE	One video can literally be repurposed into any type of content: written word, audio, or images (which we'll discuss next!).
WHO'S CRUSHING IT	Casey Neistat (YouTube: CaseyNeistat)
	Charli D'amelio (TikTok: @charlidamelio)
	Javier Vidana (YouTube: Javier Vidana)
	Ryan Read (TikTok: @ryanreadthrive)
	GaryVee (Instagram: @garyvee)
	Lizy Hoeffer Irvine (YouTube: Lizy Hoeffer)
	Ninja (Twitch: Ninja)

CONTENT TYPE IV: IMAGES

You glance down at your watch, and it's 7:42 a.m. You've had a good workout. You sit down on a gym bench to take a two-minute break before heading out. You "like" a few photos on Instagram. Then you grab your bag, slam your locker door shut, and head for your car. You wave to the gym staff on your way out, and a poster catches your eye; it sports one of your favorite celebrities advertising a new protein shake.

As you drive to the grocery store to grab a few things, you notice the billboard of a local lawyer advertising their services. You stop at the store and a fitness magazine steals your attention, so you toss it into your basket.

On your way to the checkout counter, you see an endcap with that same protein shake you saw advertised back at the gym, and you grab one before checking out, because it now feels familiar.

That's the power of images.

IMAGES: THE BASICS

While images may be easy to create, they're probably the hardest to master, and many businesses never put in the effort this type of content deserves. Even with Instagram, billboards, magazines, Pinterest, and other visually charged media, images are still undervalued. When we drive, when we scroll, when we shop, or when we do nearly anything, our eyes are scanning and consuming. Crucially, when we talk about images, we are referring to still images, not video. Video requires more single-focused attention.

Essentially, images break down into two distinct categories: graphic design (or simply "design") and photography. Photography is mostly about the capturing of an already-present image and then conveying it, whereas design has more to do with organizing and arranging graphics, font, and even art. Obviously, there's overlap between the two categories, but an expert photographer and an expert graphic designer don't necessarily share the same skillset.

Yes, People *Do* Judge a Book by Its Cover

First impressions are everything. Stopping someone from the rapid pace of scrolling, posting, and clicking is difficult and valuable. Studies reveal that attention moves within seconds of boredom. If a marketer misses that small window, the looker's attention moves on. The first thing someone sees, on a cover, on a website, or on the street, determines whether their eyes—and brain—stay or move.

For instance, without any other information, someone browsing at the bookstore may purchase the book with the best cover, if it relates at all to their topic of choice. The same is true with Instagram, car purchases, and nearly any other decision. Our eyes and brains lock on to that which is most aesthetically pleasing. Stopping someone, then, becomes the first objective.

DESIGN ALWAYS MATTERS

Interestingly, even with writing, design matters.

Consider Twitter, which is a text-centric platform designed to capture attention through the written word. Even there, the best-performing and viral tweets are almost always aesthetically pleasing, with lots of white space, a poetic appearance, and a general appeal to the eyes. So, yes, even on a microblogging platform, design matters. That's why if you happen to be especially skilled at creating and designing things that people love to look at, you could make an entire career out of this one skill.

IMAGES: HOW TECH CAN HELP

The cost of visual content creation has dropped significantly. An iPad Pro, for instance, allows an artist unlimited attempts at the perfect drawing or painting. Decades ago, that same artist would have limited options because of the high cost of materials, such as canvas, paper, paints, and brushes. Now, experimentation is cheap, allowing for accelerated iteration and innovation.

IMAGES: PROS AND CONS

Images grab attention at lightning speed, a definite positive. It takes less than one second to steal someone's eyes, and once you do, you can then get them to do anything: click on a post, watch a video, read a blurb, or consider a purchase.

The negative flip side is apparent: it's easy to lose someone's visual attention.

Also, because of the insane amount of competition for eyes, it is difficult to maintain consistent, high-quality visual content.

BASEBALL CARD FOR IMAGES

CONSIDER THIS IF...	If you like being behind the scenes, you may enjoy creating images, as you don't need to directly interact with your customer.
MY BOLD PREDICTION	Artificial intelligence (AI) and machine learning (ML) will increasingly lower the cost of design, but technology will never replace human creativity. So, in the near future, everyone's smartphone will be able to create professional-quality stills in seconds, at least in terms of lighting and color. But the most creative photos and graphics (the ones that have incredibly well-developed ideas) will continue to dominate, and these will always require human creativity.
WHY I LOVE THIS	Most businesses will eventually need someone who can create visually stunning designs, whether for their logo, book cover, CD case, packaging, photography, or website. So, if *you* learn how to steal attention with images, you can take that skill with you into any business venture.
HOW TO REPURPOSE	Once you have mastered this content type—images (still graphics and photos that don't move)—you can usually make the jump into videography, because many of the components (such as lighting) are the same.
WHO'S CRUSHING IT	Chris Do (Instagram: @thechrisdo)
	Andrick Aviles (Instagram: @andrickaviles)
	Adam J Kurtz (Instagram: @adamjk)
	Dani Donovan (Instagram: @danidonovan)
	Dinosaur (Instagram: @DinomanJ)
	Beeple (Instagram: @beeple_crap)
	Stefanie Lugo (Instagram: @bryceandstefanie)

~~~~~~

So, those are the four main types of content.

You don't need to create all of them. You'll need to find a *niche* within these types, one that uses ingredients of one or more of the four main types of content (written word, audio, video, and images), and then point that at the right group of people.

So, yes, that was a lot of information about content, much of which may not apply to you. But hey, you just took an entire crash course on marketing. Now, instead of trying to master all of marketing, go onto the next chapter to find your Content Niche, please.

SUMMARY

Businesses often spread efforts thin on a variety of marketing efforts. Smart marketing ensures that efforts focus on gaining the attention of those who are most likely to say yes to your business, in the easiest possible way. People spend their attention on four main categories of content: written word, audio, video, and images. Understanding how these foundational content types interact is crucial for today's entrepreneurs. Importantly, you don't need to *use* all of these content types, just understand them so you can use some or all of the ingredients to formulate your own Content Niche.

Key takeaways:

- Smart marketing seeks attention from people who are likely to say yes, using the easiest possible method. It's not about trying to reach all people. It's about trying to reach the right people.
- The written word is often the easiest place to start for many entrepreneurs. It's inexpensive and easy to produce, and any writing skills developed will be useful elsewhere, as the written word, particularly copywriting, is used for nearly everything in marketing, from title creation to naming a product.
- Audio has found a new golden age via podcasting. Businesses can take advantage of the passivity with which podcasting is consumed.
- Video is more difficult to produce, but the easiest to repurpose. Once you have created video content, you can easily repurpose the content into a podcast, take snippets for quotes, or create still images and post them on social media.
- Images are everywhere. The skillset necessary to create captivating images, whether photographs or graphic design, is always in demand.
- Congratulations. You just completed an entire (crash) course in marketing.

CHAPTER 8

Choose a Content Niche

You just learned about the four main types of content, the big, overarching categories that contain everything. Now, it's time to find your specialized Content Niche within those main categories, or a combination of them.

I know.

It can be a bit intimidating when it's actually time to commit to a Content Niche. So to get you started, I'm going to walk you through how Harry and Rachel would use the Content Niche equation. That way, you'll have some practice before you find your own Content Niche.

Remember, the Content Niche equation looks like this:

Content Niche = You + Your Business + Your Customer –
The Competition

Our first stop is with Harry, the trail-running machine.

HARRY'S CONTENT NICHE

We left Harry after he found his Biz-Niche—selling high-quality breathable hats designed for trail runners.

To find his Content Niche, he should consider himself first—his personal likes and dislikes, his quirks, and hobbies and special skills. This guy loves all things trail running, everything from packing his bag to lacing his shoes. He doesn't like writing. Also, he's a bit extraverted and likes to gab.

Harry's business is a bit visual, as his hats need to be seen for their value to be understood.

As far as competition goes, blogs are the primary content available to trail runners.

Harry's customer is a trail runner who wants to experience new trails and new products available to them.

After considering everything, Harry believes a video series focusing on new trails and new products would be a great form of content for trail runners. Other trail runners would enjoy the video, because they're always trying to get a feel for a trail before they try it themselves. Also, Harry believes trail runners are always wanting to see someone else try a product before they themselves commit to it, and watching Harry's hats out on the trail would show off how durable they are. The best part is, to develop video content, Harry can keep doing what he loves: running trails, discovering new areas, and finding the best gear. He'll just do all those things with a camera. (Plus, since he likes to talk, video fits nicely!)

Put everything together, and Harry's Content Niche looks like this:

HARRY	He loves trail running. He's talkative. He doesn't enjoy writing.
HARRY'S BUSINESS	His hats need to be seen to be understood.
HARRY'S CUSTOMER	His customer is an avid trail runner who wants to experience new trails and find new, quality products.
MINUS THE COMPETITION	The most widely available content for trail runners is blogs.
HARRY'S CONTENT NICHE	*A video series directed at trail runners.*

RACHEL'S CONTENT NICHE

Remember, Rachel is selling a service, and her Biz-Niche is selling real estate services to single moms in Charleston.

Rachel enjoys building long-term relationships with others.

She's a single mom with two teenage kids. Rachel is really interested in her city's overall business development and job market. Since her divorce, she's been extremely open and honest about the struggles of single parenthood. (Other single parents often tell her, "Wow! You're so honest.")

Most of Rachel's real estate competitors focus on the visual aspects of selling property—so the industry is saturated with images of homes, drone shots, etc. While Rachel's real estate business *seems* visual on the surface, Rachel knows that her Biz-Niche is more about *connecting* with local single moms, as most of Rachel's customers are other women with whom she's built a relationship over time.

So, where does that put Rachel? She decides to create her own podcast, interviewing local women. This approach helps Rachel engage with potential buyers, whom she invites as potential guests on her show. She gets to build longer relationships with her podcast guests than she would if she sent out a flyer or had a simple commercial or put out a gazillion pictures, like most of her competitors do. Plus, a podcast helps Rachel build connections with local listeners, who could also be customers.

RACHEL	She enjoys building long-term relationships. She also loves being open and honest about the struggles of single parenthood.
RACHEL'S BUSINESS	Her real estate business depends on her ability to build trust with potential homebuyers.
RACHEL'S CUSTOMER	Local women looking to buy a home with someone they trust and feel has their best interest at heart.
MINUS THE COMPETITION	Other real estate agents focus on images and drone videos.
RACHEL'S CONTENT NICHE	*An interview-based podcast directed at local women.*

YOUR CONTENT NICHE

Okay, so you've seen a couple examples of a Content Niche in action, and now it's time to find yours.

Note: there are blank copies of this form in the back of the book if you want to create more drafts of your Content Niche. You can also download additional blank copes at SkylerIrvine.com/nicheplease.

YOU	What skills, experiences, and natural advantages do you have, and what are your interests, passions, hobbies, personality traits, quirks, etc.?
YOUR BUSINESS	What makes your business unique? Also, does your business lend itself to a particular sensory experience? For example, are you selling something that must be seen, worn, heard, or tasted?
YOUR CUSTOMER	What are the demographics of your customer? (Do they come from a particular age group, are they male or female, are they located within a specific region, what's their income level, etc.)
MINUS THE COMPETITION	Subtract the type of content that your competition is already making.
YOUR CONTENT NICHE	*The specific type of content you create, based on you, your business, your customer, minus the competition.*

A FEW TIPS ON FINDING YOUR CONTENT NICHE

Okay, if you found yourself getting a little stuck, don't worry. I have a few last tips for you that may help you find your Content Niche:

1. You Are Impossible to Replicate

One of the main reasons I tell people to use their superpowers is because no one can beat you at being you. You are your most marketable, least replicate-able asset. So use it.

DIRECT YOUR CONTENT

Notice that in both Harry's case and Rachel's case, their Content Niche isn't just unique in what type of content, but also in *who* it's directed toward. Writing in the "directed at..." portion at the end of your own Content Niche helps you remember to constantly orient every piece of content in the right direction to ensure your focus stays narrow.

(Also, remember that the most valuable superpowers are often pushed into hobbies. So, if you're wondering what you are good at, consider your hobbies!)

2. Circle Important Words

Whether you make your own or use mine, actually *write* inside of a Content Niche chart.

Once you've filled in you, your business, your customer, and your competition, go back through and circle the one to two key words that stand out for each answer. Usually, those key words will give you an idea of your Content Niche!

3. Expand the Definition of "Competition"

Competition means anyone who's selling what you're selling, but it also means competition for attention of the same *customer*. So, if you're selling a one-of-a-kind product, you may not have "competition" in the traditional sense, but, likely, someone is trying to steal attention from the same customer you are hoping to attract.

4. You Could Create a New Content Type

Often, you can combine multiple hobbies, skills, or resources to create an entirely new type of content. For instance, in 2018, a journalist named Shea Serrano wrote a bunch of essays about his favorite topic—the sitcom *Scrubs*. He asked an artistic friend to create illustrations for each of his essays. Then, he combined the essays and illustrations into a ninety-page PDF and asked all his fans to buy this "book." And many of them did.

I'm not sure anyone had ever created illustrated essays based on TV sitcoms before Shea Serrano did, but that didn't stop him. He combined all his interests—writing, journalism, and TV—to create an entirely new type of content, and he crushed it.

Whether you are selling a product or a service, a superpower that combines multiple skills to create an entirely new category can help propel you, so don't be afraid to create a new type of content as your Content Niche!

5. If You're Neutral, Let the Market Nudge You

If you don't feel like you have any natural superpowers or

talents at anything in particular, that's okay. Let your customer guide your Content Niche. Sometimes you just need to get started on something.

~~~~~~

Hopefully, each of the preceding tips helped you finalize a Content Niche that is perfect for you, your business, and your customer. Be creative, have fun, and revisit your Content Niche if you don't feel like you've quite nailed it yet. Remember, there are extra charts for you in the back of the book to help you find any niches.

Now that you're armed with the process for finding both a Biz-Niche and a Content Niche, you could start posting content immediately, but I highly suggest you first read about your Media Niche, please.

SUMMARY

You just found your Content Niche. You're incredible! Revisit it often, until you are able to narrow it to one type of content, even if it's a combination of other types of content, directed at the right people, your customers. Once you've narrowed your Content Niche, you're able to consistently create content that is unique to you and your business and that's directed at your customer.

Key takeaways:

- Harry's Content Niche: a video series directed at trail runners.
- Rachel's Content Niche: an interview-based podcast directed at local women.
- You just worked through a chapter on finding your second niche, your Content Niche. You're almost done! One more niche to go.

Part IV

Your Media Niche

CHAPTER 9

The Three Wheres

Once upon a time, someone read my niching book. They found their Biz-Niche and a Content Niche. Then they instantly found happiness and riches.

The end.

Okay, not quite. But you are pretty close to finding success doing what you love.

The last thing you need to find is your Media Niche.

WHAT IS A MEDIA NICHE?

Your Media Niche is the specific social media platform, like YouTube, Twitter, or TikTok, where you post all your content. So, if your Content Niche is a video series directed at coffee drinkers, then your Media Niche could be YouTube, Dailymotion, TikTok, Facebook, LinkedIn, or anywhere that allows you to post video. Or if posting nature pictures directed at world travelers is your Content Niche, then your Media Niche could be Instagram, Facebook, or anywhere that allows you to post pictures.

Just like with your other niches, to start, you want to focus on using *one* social media platform, or one Media Niche.

If you recall the Wine Guy, GaryVee, it helps to understand the relationship between the Content and Media Niches. GaryVee's Content Niche was a daily online video series about wine directed at non-fancy wine drinkers. From there, GaryVee's *Media* Niche took about .02 seconds to find. The obvious place to post his video series was YouTube. For many entrepreneurs and businesses, their Media Niche is equally obvious. Often, as they're creating their Content Niche, the Media Niche is creeping up. But sometimes it's not quite so obvious. There may be several different Media Niches you could use to post your content, and they may all seem equally enticing. If you're in that boat, I have a process that will help you determine the best-fit Media Niche, the place where you can post your content. It's called the three wheres of your Media Niche.

THE THREE WHERES

The three wheres are pretty simple; they are:

- Where works?
- Where's trending?
- Where's novel?

When you ask yourself all these questions, it becomes pretty easy to see which Media Niche, which social media platform, works the best for you.

Let's break each element of the three wheres down:

WHERE WORKS?

The fundamental question an entrepreneur answers with this element is, *Which social media platform is a natural advantage for my Content Niche?* Sometimes, as it was with GaryVee, there is exactly one Media Niche that fits perfectly with your Content Niche. Other times, there are multiple answers to this question.

WHERE'S TRENDING?

Where's trending simply refers to that—which social media platforms are trending?

But this question gets a bit tricky, because it refers to what's trending in popular culture *and* to what's trending with your customer specifically.

For example, if Tik-Tok is the most widely used platform, but *your* customer is using YouTube more, you should include both answers to this question. In the end, you could take one of two strategies: You could follow your customer's attention to YouTube, or you could anticipate that your customer's attention will eventually move to TikTok, and be there first. Being first comes with its own set of challenges and its own rewards, which we'll dive into a little more in Chapter 10. For now, just include both answers—what's trending with either pop culture and/or your customer.

WHERE'S NOVEL?

Where's novel refers to the platforms that your competition is not utilizing right now, at least not in the way you could utilize it with your content. Again, this takes some creative thought. You're competing for attention, particularly with your audience. So, when you're looking for a novel platform, you aren't just looking for one that's not being used, you're looking for one where *your* Content Niche would be novel. Remember, your Content Niche isn't just "video," or "blog," it's a type of content with a particular focus on a particular group of people. So, often, the answer to "Where's novel?" may include social media platforms that many businesses are using, but not in the way you would use it.

When you put all three wheres together, it looks like this:

WHERE WORKS?	Which social media platforms offer a natural advantage for your Content Niche?
WHERE'S TRENDING?	1: Which social media platforms are trending with your customer?
	2: Which social media platforms are trending in popular culture?
WHERE'S NOVEL?	Which social media platforms is your competition not utilizing?
YOUR MEDIA NICHE	*The specific social media platform where you post your content.*

Note: More blank tables are available at the back of the book, and you can download additional copies at SkyerIrvine.com/nicheplease.

You'll immediately notice that the three wheres of your Media Niche behave differently than the processes you use to find your Biz-Niche and Content Niche. With the three wheres, you are looking for overlap with the three questions. Often, there will be one social media platform that pops up in each where, making your Media Niche easy to find. Other times, your Media Niche may only pop up in two out of the three where questions. That's okay; trust the process, and trust your gut. Remember, the three wheres are there to help you be creative, not spit out an exact answer. So, in the words of Captain Barbossa, the three wheres of your Media Niche are "more what you'd call 'guidelines' than actual rules."

So, in the words of Captain Barbossa, the three wheres of your Media Niche are "more what you'd call 'guidelines' than actual rules."

Then, right after he said that, Captain Barbossa said something that eventually got cut from the script of *Pirates of the Caribbean*:

"Niche, please."

SUMMARY

Your Media Niche is the final niche in the niche trifecta. Simply, the Media Niche is the one specific social media platform you use to distribute your content. Finding a Media Niche requires creativity, observation of marketplace trends, and a clear focus on what social media platform will ultimately lead to more business.

Key takeaways:

- Your Media Niche is the specific social media platform where you post your content.
- The three wheres of your Media Niche:
  - → **Where works?** Which social media platform is a natural advantage for your Content Niche?
  - → **Where's trending?** 1: Which social media platforms

are trending with your customer? 2: Which social media platforms are trending in popular culture?

→ **Where's novel?** Which social media platforms is your competition not utilizing?

CHAPTER 10

Putting All the Niches Together

You don't have to do anything alone.

Yes, it's time to use the three wheres to find that final niche, your Media Niche. Then, you'll put that final piece of the niche puzzle with your other two niches so you can have the perfect niche triumvirate.

But you don't have to do it by yourself: Harry and Rachel are here to go with you. In fact, they're going to go first, so you can see how they do it.

Let's start with Harry the hat guy.

HARRY'S THREE NICHES

As a reminder, here are Harry's other two niches:

- Harry's Biz-Niche: selling high-quality breathable hats designed for trail runners.
- Harry's Content Niche: a video series directed at trail runners.

Now, for Harry's Media Niche, he needs to fill in the three wheres.

First, he considers where works. YouTube, Facebook, Instagram, and TikTok all offer video services.

Next, Harry answers the question, "Where's trending?" TikTok is on fire in 2021 in pop culture. But dedicated trail runners are usually a little older, putting them about one social media platform behind the movement of pop culture. More likely, Harry's customer is using YouTube and Instagram.

Finally, Harry believes YouTube and TikTok are probably the most novel platforms for him to post trail-running content.

Harry puts it all together, and here's what he comes up with:

WHERE WORKS?	YouTube, Facebook, Instagram, TikTok.
WHERE'S TRENDING?	TikTok is trending with pop culture, and YouTube and Instagram are trending with Harry's customers.
WHERE'S NOVEL?	YouTube, TikTok.
HARRY'S MEDIA NICHE	*YouTube.*

In Harry's case, YouTube shows up in every single box. So, he chooses that as his Media Niche, but there isn't an absolute "right answer" here. Harry could have chosen a number of viable options, such as TikTok, which also showed up in every answer in the box. This is where Harry will need to decide if he'll want to "beat" his customer to the TikTok platform, and wait for them to show up there, or if he wants to follow his customer to where their attention already is, on YouTube. The answer may be one thing today, and another tomorrow. Today, Harry chooses to follow his customer to YouTube.

Now, let's check out Rachel's Media Niche.

RACHEL'S THREE NICHES

Let's recap Rachel's Biz-Niche and Content Niche:

- Rachel's Biz-Niche: selling homes to female homebuyers in Charleston, South Carolina.
- Rachel's Content Niche: an interview-based podcast directed at local women.

Finding Rachel's Media Niche requires considerably less creativity. Podcasts can only be distributed on a limited number of highly specialized platforms designed specifically to host podcasts. Further, as of 2021, almost all podcasting platforms work in exactly the same way. They're so similar, in fact, you actually post your audio files to an extremely inexpensive third-party service that then distributes your podcast across any or all podcast platforms, simultaneously.

So, Rachel doesn't have to "choose" a Media Niche. She gets to utilize all podcast platforms without any additional effort. I call this sort of bonus a "Media Niche BOGO."

Rachel's Media Niche chart looks like this:

WHERE WORKS?	Apple Podcasts, Google Podcasts, Spotify.
WHERE'S TRENDING?	Spotify is the most up-and-coming platform, followed by Apple Podcasts and Google Podcasts.
WHERE'S NOVEL?	Spotify is likely the most underutilized.
RACHEL'S MEDIA NICHE	*Apple Podcasts, Google Podcasts, Spotify.*

THE CONTENT-MEDIA DANCE

There's one more thing I want to tell you before you uncover your Media Niche.

MEDIA NICHE BOGOS

In general, you should choose exactly one Media Niche, which ensures you don't get overwhelmed with options. But here's the good news: sometimes, after you pick your Media Niche, you get a BOGO. Podcasting provides an excellent example of Media Niche BOGOs.

As we discussed, a podcast is nearly 100 percent identical, regardless of whether it's on Spotify, Google Podcasts, or Apple Podcasts, so you can use a service to do a one-and-done upload. You "post" your content on a behind-the-scenes service, and it instantly appears on every podcast platform. This is what I call a Media Niche BOGO. Why not take it?

Eventually, podcasting platforms may differentiate themselves logistically, by content, or by market, making it less practical or more difficult to cross-distribute. But for now, you get a BOGO with podcasting.

In this book, I've separated the Content and Media Niches, in that sequential order. But in reality, one informs the other, and there's significant overlap between the two. Plus, it's the twenty-first century. There's equality now, and the Media Niche doesn't always have to follow. Sometimes, it leads. That's what happened with GaryVee—he saw YouTube coming up, and he thought, *I'm going to be an early adopter of that platform. How can I use it to benefit my business?* In that way, GaryVee led with his Media Niche (YouTube) and let his Content Niche follow.

You can do the same.

You may spot a social media platform that's perfect for your business, and want to adopt it as your Media Niche, before you even consider your Content Niche. If that's you, go for it.

Also, the two niches can really dance together, where one leads, then follows, then leads again. For instance, if you choose "a blog directed at families traveling internationally" as your Content Niche, but then choose Twitter as your Media Niche, you may need to adjust your Content Niche slightly to "a *microblog* directed at families traveling internationally." In this way, the two niches are helping refine each other, and you, the entrepreneur, dance between the two to come up with the perfect Content and Media niches.

YOUR THREE NICHES

You've read the book, and you've followed Harry and Rachel. Now, it's your turn.

You've already written the first draft of your Biz-Niche and your Content Niche. But here's some fresh space to write them down again, along with your Media Niche.

These three niches together act as a powerful trifecta, jump-starting a new business or providing immense clarity to a pre-existing company. Remember, the most important aspect of your business, your content, and your media will always be you. That's the magic. I can give you all the other ingredients, but without your uniqueness, the charts below would lack substance, appearing identical for every person and every business.

As always, you can check the back of the book for blank niche charts, or download more copies at SkylerIrvine.com/nicheplease.

WHO	Who do you want to reach with your product or service?
WHAT	What action(s) do you want them to take?
WHY	Why would they choose you over the competition?
YOUR BIZ-NICHE	*The narrow focus of selling your product or service to a subcategory of people with low competition.*

YOU	What skills, experiences, and natural advantages do you have, and what are your interests, passions, hobbies, personality traits, quirks, etc.?
YOUR BUSINESS	What makes your business unique? Also, does your business lend itself to a particular sensory experience? For example, are you selling something that must be seen, worn, heard, or tasted?
YOUR CUSTOMER	What are the demographics of your customer? (Do they come from a particular age group, are they male or female, are they located within a specific region, what's their income level, etc.)
MINUS THE COMPETITION	Subtract the type of content that your competition is already making.
YOUR CONTENT NICHE	*The specific type of content you create, based on you, your business, your customer, minus the competition.*

WHERE WORKS?	Which social media platforms offer a natural advantage for your Content Niche?
WHERE'S TRENDING?	1: Which social media platforms are trending with your customer? 2: Which social media platforms are trending in popular culture?
WHERE'S NOVEL?	Which social media platforms is your competition not utilizing?
YOUR MEDIA NICHE	*The specific social media platform where you post your content.*

FIVE SECRETS OF YOUR MEDIA NICHE

Oftentimes, there's one perfect Media Niche for you and your business; other times, nothing jumps out. If nothing's landing, here are a few "secrets" that can help uncover your Media Niche:

SECRET 1: SPOT TRENDS IN APP STORES

Regularly monitor the top social media apps in the various app stores, find the trending apps, and consider becoming an early adopter.

SECRET 2: BE YOUNG AT HEART

Tomorrow's adults are today's kids. So, whatever kids are into today, adults will be into tomorrow. Also, nostalgia remains undefeated. Even when something (like Super Nintendo) goes out of style, it will always come back.

SECRET 3: SOCIETY SWINGS TO EXTREMES

"Skyler, which platform is going to be the biggest?!" I don't know. But I *do* know that when the market becomes oversaturated with one type of content, people bounce to another. So, as video becomes more and more popular, it also becomes less novel, setting up society for a massive move to a different type of content.

This swinging effect also shows up in more nuanced ways. For instance, millennials flocked to Instagram to display perfectly captured stills of immaculate settings and perfect body types. Gen Zers stayed visual, but instead of pictures of perfection, they popularized TikTok, embracing the expressiveness of dance, capturing every bit of an individual's quirkiness, sans the perfection of Instagram.

SECRET 4: SIZE DOESN'T MATTER

Unless your goal is popularity, increasing the size of your audience for numbers' sake isn't the goal. Your marketing efforts, including your Content and Media Niches, should be pointed at a strategy that tracks to results for you and your business. It doesn't make sense to capture the attention of 90 percent of the world if all your customers are in that last 10 percent.

SECRET 5: FOCUS ON HIGH ROI

Remember to focus on the highest return for your marketing efforts. There is an ever-growing number of platforms you *could* use. Don't focus on the new and the shiny. Instead, find the platform that delivers the most reward for the lowest investment.

"WHAT IF I'M THE FIRST?"

Pioneering is difficult.

When you're niching, you're always "first" at some level. But sometimes, you're truly a first. For instance, maybe you've come up with an entirely new Content Niche no one's ever utilized, or you want to use a Media Niche in a way it's never been used. Or, perhaps, you want to "beat" your customer or the general public by being an early adopter of a new social media platform or app. These could all be smart moves. You just need to understand the nuances and complexities of how being a true first actually work.

So, let's go over what it means to be first, and what implications this could have on your business.

Overall, there are three main ways you can be first:

- You could create a new type of Content Niche. Shea Serrano essentially did this by creating illustrated essays directed at TV fans.

- You could use a Media Niche in a new way. If someone decided to use TikTok to post snippets of their writing, that would be a unique way to use a Media Niche. Or, if an architect decided to share blueprints on Instagram, they would likely be one of the first architects utilizing Instagram for blueprints.
- Be an early adopter of a Media Niche. You could be the first by moving to a platform (or app) ahead of the wave of the general population. In this way, you would be set up to rise with the popularity of the platform. Alternatively, you may not be among the first overall to adopt a new platform, but you could be the first from your industry to adopt a platform.

In each case above, being the first has similar advantages and potential downsides. For one, businesses that are first are likely to only have a small audience, at least initially. But chances are, they'll monopolize the attention as a platform, subject, or content becomes more popular.

Similarly, when you're alone, or way ahead of the curve, you set yourself up to be the expert in case the tide turns. For instance, if you're one of the first to discuss a new idea or revive an old one, you could hit expert status overnight, just because no one else knows the subject as well as you do. Consider someone who starts a video series on You-

Tube directed at serious Ninja Turtles fans. We'll call him Connor. Connor's video series serves a very specific group of people where few (if any) competitors exist. Most people won't watch Connor's series, but a few dedicated Turtles fans probably will. For a while, Connor's video series will enjoy a small but captive audience. But if a Ninja Turtle movie or cartoon series suddenly explodes in pop culture, and the audience for Ninja Turtles grows exponentially overnight, the media will look for someone with subject-matter expertise. Connor will suddenly become a sought-after expert.

Is that extremely likely to happen? Not necessarily, but, as you will see in the next chapter, it could happen.

In any case, the advantage of being first is that the pond is smaller, and the smaller the pond, the easier it is to be a big fish. Of course, the flip side is also true: you're in a small pond.

~~~~~

You did it. You niched. Thrice. (That's a fancy word that means three times.)

You now have three niches that will orient your business to achieve maximum results. You have successfully narrowed your focus, and you're set up to grow your reach. So, the next time a pesky thought tries to intimidate you about social media marketing, just say, "Niche, please."

SUMMARY

When a business finds all three niches, they are positioned to reach their maximum potential. Each niche works together to help the other, and as focus narrows, efforts become more effective.

Key takeaways:

- Harry's Media Niche: YouTube.
- Rachel's Media Niche: Apple Podcasts, Google Podcasts, Spotify. (Rachel is the recipient of a Media Niche BOGO. These are additional social media platforms on which you can cross-distribute your content, with no additional effort.)
- There is a "dance" between the Content and Media Niches. You may find either niche first, or even both simultaneously, as one niche informs and refines the other.
- Finding your Media Niche requires creativity. Use these five secrets to help:
  1. Spot trends in app stores.
  2. Be young at heart.
  3. Society swings to extremes.
  4. Size doesn't matter.

5. Focus on high ROI.

🔊 Being first has its advantages. Being an early adopter of a platform, or an early adopter of a type of content or subject matter on a platform, or one of the first to discuss or revive a topic, has its advantages. If the platform, content type, or subject matter gets a boost from popular culture, you will be well-positioned to rise, respectively.

🔊 You found all three of your own niches. You can use them to take over the world.

A BONUS FOR BEING FIRST

No matter what kind of "first" you are, you run the possibility that others will contact you about using a platform in a similar manner. For instance, if you're one of the first coffee shops to effectively use Snapchat, other coffee shops could become clients of yours on how to use Snapchat to market their coffee shops.

Part V

`,`,`,`,`,`,`,`,`,`,`,

"What Do I Post?"

CHAPTER 11

Limit Yourself

You've found all three of your niches. Now, it's time to post something online, to say something.

"But Skyler! What do I post?" you may ask.

That's a great question.

Ask Charli D'Amelio.

In the summer of 2019, a teenager named Charli D'Amelio joined an only moderately known social media app called TikTok. She was only fifteen, but other TikTok users loved her.

She was a competitive dancer from Norwalk, Connecticut, and TikTok's dance focus was a perfect fit for her. When she joined, TikTok wasn't center stage in national attention. But a few months later, the app started picking up viral steam in teenage pop culture. And when TikTok blew up, so did Charli D'Amelio. (In fact, some say TikTok owes part of *its* popularity to her.)

By her sixteenth birthday, she had passed up every other influencer on the platform, creating an incredible fan base of over fifty-five million followers. She had attention. A lot of it. By comparison, Tom Cruise had around five million followers on Instagram. So in the spring of 2020, Charli D'Amelio apparently commanded eleven times more attention within the preteen and teen demographic than the guy who has starred in half a dozen and counting *Mission: Impossible* movies.

With her audience, Charli D'Amelio isn't merely popular— she's a sensation.

But her success didn't come overnight.

She was, for a time, on an app called Musical.ly, a precursor to TikTok. She also had an Instagram presence. But when she moved to TikTok, her life changed. She understood the content her fans wanted, and she has consistently delivered tons of that exact content.

Now, she has 100 million fans, and she's grown from

making short dance videos with her friends to being in Super Bowl commercials with Jennifer Lopez.

Be like Charli D'Amelio.

LIMITS ILLUMINATE THE PATH

Charli D'Amelio is the undisputed "Queen of TikTok."

Anyone who's into fun, short dances pays attention to Charli D'Amelio, and she's able to impact people's decisions.

Certainly, she was a somewhat lucky beneficiary of TikTok being pushed into the spotlight, so her audience grew exponentially. She was a true first, and she caught the wave at the perfect time. But importantly, she would have been successful within her niche crowd of lovers of fun dance moves, regardless of whether TikTok became as popular as it did. She found a niche crowd, commanded their attention, and grew her reach.

You want to command that level of attention. To do that, you must be considered an expert: the go-to authority on an area of expertise. Marketers call these respected experts "thought leaders." You don't have to be the first to a platform, and command attention from 100 million people, but you do want to be the Queen (or King) of a specific subject matter with a specific audience. When you become that Royal, you are then able to command attention and influence decisions.

Now, to achieve expert status, and become a thought leader, you must both *know* a lot and *post* a lot. Guess what? You have that first part—know a lot—covered.

You already know a lot about your thing. In the same way Rachel is an expert on houses in Charleston, and Harry's a thought leader on trail-running hats, you're a thought leader or expert on ___. (Insert your thing in that blank!)

From there, armed with your expertise, the goal is to post a lot, to frequently share what you know with everyone else on social media. Frequently posting quality content is what separates an unknown genius from a respected thought leader who commands attention.

So, know a lot, post a lot.

But wait. How do I post a lot, Skyler? That's the question I had at the beginning of this chapter!?

Yes. That's the key question. And here's the kicker: to go from someone who's perhaps never made a social media post to someone who posts a lot, you need to do one counterintuitive thing. You need to take all the possibilities of what you could say, all the ways you could create that content...

And limit yourself.

Think about it—while some entrepreneurs are wondering what they should post online, guess who never asks themselves that question?

Charli D'Amelio. Shea Serrano. GaryVee.

They already know *exactly* what to post, because every time they think about social media, they have limits:

When GaryVee thought about producing content for *Wine Library TV*, he knew he'd be posting irreverent videos on YouTube about wine.

When Shea Serrano looks at his phone, he knows he'll be posting microblogs on his Twitter.

When Charli D'Amelio considers making a video, she knows she'll be posting dance videos between one and sixty seconds long for users who are interested in dance on TikTok.

See how much easier that is? By limiting themselves to very narrow lists of possibilities, smart marketers already know what they'll be posting today, tomorrow, and for the foreseeable future. They illuminate the pathway from themselves to Royalty by making the pathway narrow and direct, allowing themselves to consistently create high volumes of quality content that track directly to results.

Your goal is similar: illuminate the path from where you are to Royalty for your area of expertise. And you illuminate that path by limiting yourself, so it's easy, clear, and fun to post your content.

Once you clarify your limits, you'll never need to wonder what you're going to post. You'll know that you simply execute on your preconceived strategy, and create content for a given set of limitations.

So, let's find your limits.

LIMITS COME FROM YOUR NICHES

Limits come from all three of your niches. Once you create these limits for your content, it becomes incredibly clear what you should post, where you should post it, and almost even how you should post it. You can find all of those limits from within your different niches.

Limits from Your Biz-Niche

First, your content must generate results for your Biz-Niche, selling your product or service to a subcategory of people. You're not looking for popularity; you're looking for results.

> You're not looking for popularity; you're looking for results.

This helps limit your content significantly. Rachel's selling homes to female homebuyers in Charleston. So, everything she posts about must track to local women who will eventually be interested in purchasing a home.

Interestingly, generating results for your business does not mean you need to post *about* your business, or even that you need to post about what you do. Instead, focusing on your business means that you need to attract people who could turn into customers. For instance, Rachel's Biz-Niche is selling homes to female homebuyers in Charleston, and her Content Niche is an interview-based podcast directed at local women. Rachel doesn't need to have 1,000 podcast episodes about females buying real estate in Charleston. She could tweak some (or even all) of her podcast episodes, and instead of focusing on real estate, she could focus on local eateries, which would probably still track to results for her, as long as listeners are still located in Charleston.

Likewise, all of *your* posts should track business results, but it isn't necessary that they all speak directly about your business or what you do.

And don't get sidetracked with amazing-sounding numbers (called vanity metrics) that speak to your ego and not business results. Far too many businesses do this. They start out well, and soon they're paying attention to the metrics, and not results. They beef up their metrics in response, only to lose their true customer's attention. To illustrate what I mean, consider this scenario:

Harry the hat guy starts his video series about trail running.

After three months, five hundred trail runners are regularly watching his video series, and he's selling plenty of hats. But he notices that his friend Andy, who also hosts a YouTube show, has five *thousand* listeners. Andy talks about pop culture. Harry wants to have more viewers, so he broadens the focus of his show to discussing national topics.

In time, Harry's viewership grows, but his sales decline, because instead of his video series delivering consistent value to trail runners, it's discussing topics that are of less interest to them. His smaller, dedicated, strategic viewer base was tracking to greater results, while the broader focus of a national show about pop culture started attracting those who weren't likely to be customers. Businesses make similar mistakes frequently by looking to vanity metrics instead of results.

There is nothing wrong with trying to grow a huge audience if that's your end goal. Influencers are selling the size of their audience, so their whole goal may be to grow an audience. Yet, for most businesses, your goal isn't a huge audience. It's an audience of the right people. So, if you're ever doubtful about a piece of content, just ask yourself, "Does this content track the results for my Biz-Niche?"

Limits from Your Content Niche

Secondly, and perhaps overly obviously, your Content Niche provides clear limits: if you're Harry and you're creating a video series directed at trail runners, you don't need to worry much about podcasting. This one's pretty easy.

Limits from Your Media Niche

Lastly, your chosen Media Niche usually provides plenty of

limits, in a couple different ways. For one, there are technical limitations to every platform. Whether you're posting blogs or pictures or videos, you have to stay within those requirements to post. Shea Serrano creates microblogs that are less than 280 characters long, because that's a technical requirement for his Media Niche, Twitter. This type of technical barrier is extremely helpful, because when you lead with it, you drown out the noise of what you "could" create, and you clarify what you must create—something within the technical limits.

But there's another type of nontechnical limit that your Media Niche provides. Most social media platforms have *cultural norms* that have developed. These provide guidelines for the type of content that will be readily consumed on a platform. For instance, Charli D'Amelio now only records her dance videos vertically, instead of horizontally, as she originally did. Why? Well, vertical videos are a cultural norm of the TikTok platform, and people will rarely watch a video that's filmed in any other way, even though horizontal video may technically be allowed.

As you look at your own Media Niche, poke around the platform just enough so you understand any of the hidden cultural norms. They're pretty easy to spot, they take little time, and you can adjust as you learn more about them.

MOVE WITH YOUR CUSTOMER

I want to be very clear: don't fall in love with a certain platform. While you do want to double down on one platform to start your marketing, you don't want to fall in love forever. This isn't a marriage.

The marketplace is littered with businesses who did just that—they learned one social media platform and refused to shift. They fell in love, and when their customer shifted their attention, the brand stayed while the attention left. That doesn't need to be you.

If your customer is shifting their attention from a platform you've mastered, take a breath and realize what you've already mastered:

You have a great product (or service).

You know how to narrow your focus.

You already have customers.

You know how to gain their attention.

Any new, competing company will still be behind you when it comes to their business and their marketing, even if they happen to know the new social media platform better than you do. You have the customers, the story, and the experience. Learn the easy part (the new platform), and then transport all your knowledge and expertise.

It would be a shame if GaryVee, Charli D'Amelio, or Shea Serrano stayed with the platforms they helped elevate, and then never moved when the attention moved.

Royalty never gets left behind.

~~~~~

Your goal is to be the Royalty of your thing, so that people pay attention to you. To get there, you must know a lot, and post a lot. You already know a lot. Now, you must post a lot. Posting seems intimidating because of all the possibilities, but when you limit yourself, the path from you to Royalty becomes instantly clear. Take that next step, and the next one, by posting within your limits. Then post again.

PURSUE CUSTOMERS NOT SIMILAR EXPERTS

Another common mistake entrepreneurs often make is creating too much content for other experts. As a result, they end up capturing the attention of people who aren't likely to buy from them.

For instance, if you're a ghostwriter who helps famous politicians and celebrities write their stories, you don't need to create content that attracts attention from *ghostwriters.* You need to create content that attracts attention from *famous politicians and celebrities.* Likewise, if you're a plumber, your customers are not other plumbers. Your customers are probably general contractors, apartment complexes, and/or homeowners.

Occasionally inviting another expert or thought leader on your show or blog, or featuring them in some way, could increase your audience or provide your customer more value. But, generally speaking, when entrepreneurs begin to court other thought leaders, they get caught up in hype and lose sight of the goal.

Again, focus on results, not other experts.

Eventually, you'll find that you've created a trail of knowledgeable posts that track to results. With enough knowledgeable posts, you're well on your way to Royalty. It all starts with limits.

So, armed with your limits, next time you don't know what to post, just say, "Niche, please."

SUMMARY

What do I post?! is a common, intimidating thought for

first-time social media marketers. Smart marketers aren't always wondering what to post because they've limited themselves. By limiting yourself, you illuminate the path to thought leadership.

Key takeaways:

- Limits illuminate the path. To get more attention, you must be seen as a thought leader (expert) with your audience. To be a thought leader, you must post a lot of quality content that is valuable to your audience. For you to consistently post a lot of content, it must be easy for you to post. The best way to make it easy to post is to limit yourself.
- You can find limits from your Biz-Niche, Content Niche, and Media Niche. Each one sets up a boundary within which your content must "fit":
  → Limits from your Biz-Niche: Results are more important than numbers. Small-business owners often get sidetracked with vanity metrics. It's better to have a small following of the right people than a large following of the wrong people.
  → Limits from your Content Niche: You're creating specific content directed at a specific audience.
  → Limits from your Media Niche: These boundaries are usually obvious or technical. However, some boundaries are less apparent, such as the cultural norms of a given platform.

❧ Move with your customer. Customers will move their attention. That's a given. When that happens, transport your knowledge and expertise into a new medium, if necessary. Remember: you already have the customers, the knowledge, the experience.

CHAPTER 12

10 Tips for Momentum

Still wondering how to get started with social media?

That's okay!

I put together a list of 10 ideas to help you get moving and keep momentum. These should help get your wheels turning, and keep you going when you get stuck.

1. START SMALL

Your first (or next) post doesn't have to be long.

It just needs to happen.

2. DON'T SWEAT THE DETAILS

People often stall out before they even get started. They start to fret about the smallest of details, like when to post, which camera to buy, and what type of software to use. But none of these details will make or break your content. Consistency will.

Focusing on the minutia is like thinking, *I want to be a swimmer like Michael Phelps, so I'm going to find out what he eats.* Each of us intuitively knows that eating isn't going to magically turn us into Olympic swimmers. The main reason Michael Phelps is an Olympic swimmer is because he swims a lot.

And that's how content works.

At some point, you just need to go for it. Be willing to fail. Exercise your superpowers. Sweat the small stuff later.

Basically, be like Michael Phelps.

3. BE YOU

Business owners often struggle with perfectionism. But you don't need to be perfect at social media to use it effectively.

Taylor Swift is one of the hottest selling artists in history because she doubles down on her superpower of transparency. She never strays from her open, honest discussion of a young woman's life. Few would say she is the greatest vocalist or even the greatest songwriter of all time. But she has attracted one of the largest fan bases of all time.

Likewise, your audience isn't going to follow you on social media because you're the most talented writer or videographer. They're going to follow you because you're honest with them, and you have something to share. So share it.

4. BE VULNERABLE

Even your embarrassments or mishaps can be hidden strengths. In fact, one of the fastest ways to create deeper connections with others is to share something that embarrasses you.

For instance, I was always embarrassed by my middle name. I made a video about it and released it online, and it really connected with my community.

5. PROVIDE VALUE

Unless you're trying to fall asleep at 4 a.m., do you watch infomercials?

Neither does anyone else.

Don't post content about how amazing your business is. Most of your content should provide immediate value for your customer.

6. KNOW RELEVANT CULTURE

Be authentic to who you are, but also understand modern practices for platforms and content.

For instance, if you're going to microblog, it pays to understand hashtags. While you don't need to change your entire writing style, throwing in a well-conceived hashtag at the bottom of your post could mean the difference between it getting shared by thousands or never even seen.

7. UNDERSTAND POLITICAL POSTS

Every time I give a talk at a conference, this question inevitably comes up: "Should I post about politics [or other controversial subjects] on social media?"

That's like asking if the beaches are better than the mountains—they are wildly different destinations, but I can't answer which one's right for you. What I can do is describe both options and let you decide.

If you post about politics or anything controversial on social media, you are likely going to alienate approximately half your audience. Simultaneously, you will probably endear yourself to the other half. Shea Serrano, the journalist, writer, and Twitter personality I mentioned in Chapter 8, knows this better than anyone.

He released a sixty-four-page "book" on his Twitter called *How to Talk to Trump Supporters*. The first page simply says, "F*** you." As you turn the pages, you soon find out that each page is filled with small one-liners, horoscopes, and satirical "quotes" directed at Trump supporters, and each is simply another way of saying "F*** you" to them. The book was a huge hit with Shea Serrano's fans, but, as you can imagine, others likely hate this message. Shea Serrano knew what he was doing when he published it—he was endearing his fan base and pushing others further away.

So, whether you should post about political or controversial topics is up to you. Just know that controversy tends to eliminate half your audience while engaging the other half.

8. REPURPOSE CONTENT

If you get stuck after you've created tons of content, try repurposing what you have into something new.

Repurposing content to a new platform, or from one type of content to another, is easy with today's technology. Blog posts and pictures can be copied and pasted across multiple platforms. Transcripts, tweets, and blog posts can be easily created from video. As a bonus, you don't even have to do this work—you could pay others to take your best, current content and repackage it into something new.

9. PIVOT WITH ONE FOOT

At some point, you'll need to pivot.

Maybe you'll need to pivot one of your niches slightly, or maybe you'll need to go back to the ground level. In basketball, even after you've picked up the ball, you can still move one foot, as long as one foot stays planted. If you pick up the ball and then try to move both feet, a referee will penalize you.

Business is pretty similar—it's best to move one foot at a time, while keeping the other planted when changes happen.

Sometimes business changes because an industry changes. Sometimes customer attention moves. Other times, an entrepreneur initiates a change. Whatever the case, just remember you can pivot one foot at a time, without starting all the way over.

I pivoted from *flipping* real estate into helping others *buy* real estate. I kept one foot planted on what I knew (real estate) and moved the other one into a new direction of helping others purchase homes. Later, after I used social media to help others in real estate, I pivoted again, leaving one foot in social media and putting the other one into a new marketing business. GaryVee pivoted in a similar way: He started *Wine Library TV*, which was a wild success. Eventually, instead of using social media to sell wine, he moved his one foot out of wine and co-founded a digital marketing company called VaynerMedia.

You can do the same.

When it's time, either because you initiate it or the market does, you can move one foot into another venture. Luckily, you get to take everything you've learned and apply it to that new pivot.

10. MAKE A TOP 10 LIST (LIKE I JUST DID!)

Here's a hack for whenever you need to get the creative wheels turning: make your own top 10 list. For example, Harry the hat guy could create a series of videos, or one long video, called *The Top 10 Trails in Colorado*. Then, he could make another series called *The Top 10 Trails Near Denver, Colorado*. He could also make a series called *The 10 Hardest Trails in Colorado*.

Creating top 10 lists for your customer helps create great content, and it also helps push you when you're stuck.

Okay, you've been given 10 tools to help you start, or get unstuck.

Now, go forth and niche, please.

SUMMARY

Starting is the hardest part of many journeys. Other times, we get stuck somewhere, and we just need to get back to the basics. Here's ten ways to gain momentum:

1. Start small.
2. Don't sweat the details.
3. Be you.
4. Be vulnerable.
5. Provide value.
6. Know relevant culture.
7. Understand political posts.
8. Repurpose content.
9. Pivot with one foot.
10. Make a top 10 list (like I just did!).

Conclusion

Fear makes entrepreneurs feel like everything they've learned about their industry and their customers is the easy part, and the hardest part is the social media.

They have it all backward.

Your skills, talents, ideas, and industry knowledge are 90 percent of the equation. Social media is the 10 percent, the easy part. You just need some keys to unlock it.

You're now holding three keys.

- Biz-Niche: When you provide a unique product (or service) to a unique customer, you'll sell more, with less effort and less competition.
- Content Niche: When you find a unique type of content

that is fun and easy for you to produce, you set yourself up for success.

- Media Niche: When you deploy your content on the right platform, you'll only need to learn a limited amount about social media to create the most impact.

As you begin your social media journey, you're going to make mistakes. You're going to say the wrong thing, or upload the wrong file, or drop the wrong link into your post. Your content may not look as polished as your competitor's. But what will win in the end is consistency, not perfection. If you continually make amazing content that serves your customer, you'll become known as a servant for your industry. People will come back to you, and you'll win in the long run. Your future customers are never going to tell you, "I picked you because your YouTube video looked like it was produced by Steven Spielberg." People will choose you because you are always there when they need you.

On that note, I'd love to stay in touch.

If you want some ongoing, easy, applicable ideas on social media marketing, you can connect with me at SkylerIrvine. com. Oh, and I have one last story for you.

Recently, someone picked up my book and read the entire thing. They followed some of the ideas, but not all of them, because hey, no one agrees with an author 100 percent, right? They were challenged, they were a little scared, and, truthfully, they may have only lightly skimmed some of the chapters. But by the end of the book, they were excited. They decided to apply some of the concepts they learned about niching down on their business offerings. Amazingly, they finished an entire book about something that originally intimidated them.

That makes them a superhero—in my book. They faced something seemingly daunting, and conquered it.

That person is you.

Acknowledgments

I want to first acknowledge you, the reader. I appreciate you because I understand you. I understand you because I am you. I wrote this book because it's the book I needed and didn't have. I know what it's like to awkwardly respond to the standard dinner party question: "So, what is it you do for work?" I know what it's like to have an idea, but no one to talk to about it in a productive way. I also know what it's like to be burdened with choices. Paralyzed with options. When you can do anything, where do you begin?

When the economy began shutting down in spring of 2020, it brought me eerily back to 2008 when I lost my corporate job and saw uncertainty everywhere I looked. I knew I didn't want to get another corporate job, but I didn't know what that truly meant until years later.

This book is the result of all my failures more than it is about any of my success. The best lessons come from failures, and if you learned anything from this book then that's your proof. I have been blessed with a lot of luck and good fortune. I was born into the perfect family with amazing parents, Lee and Jo-Ann. Growing up, I learned so much trying to emulate and impress my older sister, Leann. I married the perfect person, Lizy, who then rewarded me with three perfect children, Anabelle, Penelope, and Calvin.

I have worked closely with so many incredible people like Daniel Brown, Danny Hoefelmann, Jillian Messina, and Ezekiel Rempel. I have been inspired by so many talented and passionate entrepreneurs and creators like Timmy Ham, Quinlin Wilhite, Randal Hedden, Ryan Read, Stefanie Lugo, Kim Dolan Leto, Aubrey Tinsley, Michael Taylor, Tim McBride, Brent Orsuga, James Patrick, Max Anderson, and so many others.

Lastly, thank you to Paul Fair, who is the sole reason that my thoughts were ever turned into words for this book. Working together from opposite sides of the country during an economic shutdown and global pandemic is even further proof that it's never been a better time to be a creator and find your niche.

Appendix I

EXTRA NICHE CHARTS

BIZ-NICHE

WHO	Who do you want to reach with your product or service?
WHAT	What action(s) do you want them to take?
WHY	Why would they choose you over the competition?
YOUR BIZ-NICHE	*The narrow focus of selling your product or service to a subcategory of people with low competition.*

CONTENT NICHE

YOU	What skills, experiences, and natural advantages do you have, and what are your interests, passions, hobbies, personality traits, quirks, etc.?
YOUR BUSINESS	What makes your business unique? Also, does your business lend itself to a particular sensory experience? For example, are you selling something that must be seen, worn, heard, or tasted?
YOUR CUSTOMER	What are the demographics of your customer? (Do they come from a particular age group, are they male or female, are they located within a specific region, what's their income level, etc.)
MINUS THE COMPETITION	Subtract the type of content that your competition is already making.
YOUR CONTENT NICHE	*The specific type of content you create, based on you, your business, your customer, minus the competition.*

MEDIA NICHE

WHERE WORKS?	Which social media platforms offer a natural advantage for your Content Niche?
WHERE'S TRENDING?	1: Which social media platforms are trending with your customer? 2: Which social media platforms are trending in popular culture?
WHERE'S NOVEL?	Which social media platforms is your competition not utilizing?
YOUR MEDIA NICHE	*The specific social media platform where you post your content.*

Appendix II

A LOOK AT TWENTY-FOUR SOCIAL MEDIA PLATFORMS

In this appendix, I've broken down what types of content you can post on twenty-four different social media platforms. (Of course, you could certainly break the "rules" and try to post a new type of content on any of these.)

A few disclaimers:

- This list is not exhaustive, as there's an infinite number of available platforms.
- This list changes rapidly. By the time you're reading this book, another major platform will likely have taken the spotlight.
- Lastly, social media platforms may evolve themselves: YouTube may transition entirely from video to podcasting, who knows?

ANCHOR	Audio, almost exclusively
	Anchor is a podcast-creation platform, purchased by Spotify in 2019, and it offers the easiest path to creating podcasts. You literally download the app to your phone, click record, then push "upload" when you're done talking. The recording posts straight to your podcast account on Spotify.
BLOGGER	Written word, almost exclusively
	Blogger is a blog platform.
BLOGSPOT	Written word, almost exclusively
	Blogspot is a blog platform.
CLUBHOUSE	Audio, almost exclusively
	Clubhouse is a new type of audio-based social networking platform that allows users to have audio discussions with each other. It was launched in 2019, and by January 2021, it was still invite-only.
FACEBOOK	Written word, audio, images, video
	Some businesses could survive only on Facebook. It is not the *best* choice for many businesses, but if I had to prescribe a one-size-fits-all for businesses, which I've tried not to do, then I would prescribe Facebook.
FLICKR	Primarily: images and written word
	Also: a dash of video and audio
	Flickr is a social media platform primarily used to share photos and join forums.
GOOGLE BUSINESS	Written word, images
	Google Business is essentially a "Facebook page" for your business that doesn't live on Facebook. Having a Google Business page won't make your business, but it's become so expected to have one that not having one could hurt you.

SOCIAL MEDIA PLATFORM

GOOGLE PODCASTS Audio, almost exclusively

Google Podcasts has become a formidable competitor in the podcasting space, but they are competing differently than Spotify. Google is using their indexing and searching capabilities to create transcripts of every podcast on their platform, so you will be able to type in a search on Google, and the results will show podcasts that contain the key words from your search.

INSTAGRAM Primarily: images and written word

Also: video is growing

Instagram is primarily an image-sharing app that was purchased by Facebook, and it has become a dominating force in the social media world.

LINKEDIN Primarily: written word

Also: images and video are quickly growing

LinkedIn's goal was to be the "Facebook for business." By 2021, they've more or less achieved that goal, as more and more professional users cling to the platform to share industry-specific content.

MEDIUM Primarily: written word

Also: images

Medium is a blog platform, geared toward curating slightly higher-quality content than other blogging platforms.

MYSPACE Written word, audio, video, images

Myspace has gone through several evolutions. It was Facebook before Facebook, and now, it's partially owned by Justin Timberlake, who's attempting to turn it into a music platform. As of 2021, he's had little success doing so.

SOCIAL MEDIA PLATFORM

PINTEREST

Primarily: images

Also: written word

Also: a dash of video and audio

Pinterest is a visual platform that allows users to "pin" lists, ideas, recipes, and images on their page.

QUORA

Written word, almost exclusively

REDDIT

Written word, images, video

SNAPCHAT

Written word, audio, images, video

Snapchat is hard to ignore, but by 2020, it plateaued in popularity. It was started as a picture-sharing mobile platform, and it's added more functionality.

SPOTIFY

Audio, almost exclusively

Spotify, already one of the most-used music platforms in the world, is on a mad dash to also become the "YouTube of podcasting." And they're well on their way. They purchased Anchor to encourage more users to create podcasts for their platform, and Spotify has also purchased various other podcasts and platforms.

TIKTOK

Video, audio

TikTok has evolved to a video-centric social media platform, geared primarily toward sharing dance videos and new music.

TUMBLR

Images, written word, video

This platform has been bought and resold by various larger companies, like Yahoo. Essentially, as of 2021, it is a giant collection of user-created "blogs," most of which are visually captivating.

TWITTER

Primarily: written word

Also: images, video, and audio (in that order)

Twitter is a "microblog" social media platform that's famous for its low character limit.

SOCIAL MEDIA PLATFORM

WECHAT	Written word, audio, video, images
	In China, this app is king. It's used for literally everything from text messaging to making payments.
WHATSAPP	Primarily: written word
	Also: images, video, audio
	WhatsApp is a text messaging platform that allows people with different device types, such as Apple or Android, to text each other. Facebook purchased the platform in 2014, and it's become wildly successful in most parts of the world. The platform has also branched out into social media, file sharing, and other areas.
WORDPRESS	Written word, images
	WordPress is a blogging platform.
YOUTUBE	Video
	Also: a dash of audio and written word
	Fun fact: YouTube originally started as an online dating service, where you uploaded your video as part of your dating profile.

About the Author

SKYLER IRVINE is the founder and CEO of RenzlerMedia, a digital production company that helps entrepreneurs and small businesses tell their unique stories and support their brands with technology and social media. He believes everyone has their own path to success, one based on distinctive ideas and interests that separate every good entrepreneur from their competition. According to Skyler, pursuing our interests allows us to turn our ideas into money and erase the line between work and play.

Skyler graduated from the University of California, Santa Barbara, with a degree in global studies and international relations. He lives in Phoenix, Arizona, with his wife and three kids.

BIZ NICHE

WHO

WHAT

WHY

YOUR BIZ-NICHE

CONTENT NICHE

YOU

YOUR BUSINESS

YOUR CUSTOMER

MINUS THE COMPETITION

YOUR CONTENT NICHE

MEDIA NICHE

WHERE WORKS?

WHERE'S TRENDING?

WHERE'S NOVEL?

YOUR MEDIA NICHE

BIZ NICHE

WHO

WHAT

WHY

YOUR BIZ-NICHE

CONTENT NICHE

YOU

YOUR BUSINESS

YOUR CUSTOMER

MINUS THE COMPETITION

YOUR CONTENT NICHE

MEDIA NICHE

WHERE WORKS?

WHERE'S TRENDING?

WHERE'S NOVEL?

YOUR MEDIA NICHE